Type 2 Diabetes Instant Pot Cookbook

5-Ingredient Affordable, Easy and Healthy Recipes for Your Instant Pot | 30-Day Meal Plan | How to Prevent, Control and Live Well with Diabetes

Pater Higher

Table of contents

Introduction

Imagine you need a frying pan, steamer, warming pot, rice cooker, and slow cooker. But you don't want to purchase all or store them in your kitchen. Then you will love instant pot. The instant pot is a perfect kitchen appliance for those who don't have much time to do exhaustive cooking but want to eat delicious and notorious food quickly and easily.

It doesn't matter if you are Keto or diabetic, you are just trying to eat healthy food; Instant pot is the answer for nutritious fast food.

Just add all your ingredients, even frozen ones, into the pot, and the result is delicious and super healthy food.

Chapter 1: Understanding the Diabetes

How to identify if you have Diabetes

Diabetes is a common chronic condition in which the blood glucose level of the body gets higher than normal. Medically, this condition is also known as hyperglycemia and is caused by eating too many carbs, skipping diabetic medicines or insulin, stress, or infections.

However, don't confuse diabetes with low blood sugar level; it is actually one of the most common complications of treatment for diabetes. When glucose level drops down, the body suffers from the condition called hypoglycemia. Just like mentioned before, a person develops hypoglycemia due to poor nutrition or taking too much diabetic medicines or insulin.

Therefore, identifying its early signs of diabetes and overall symptoms is very essential as it can help a person in treating and controlling diabetes earlier before it leads to life-threatening health complications including heart stroke, coronary diseases, nerve damage, kidney diseases, eye diseases, seizures, and sexual problems.

The symptoms of diabetes include:

- Feeling hungry

Our body break downs food into glucose, a simple sugar, which is then used as a fuel and pass to the cell from the bloodstream. The individuals that have developed diabetes, the glucose isn't delivered much to the cell. Therefore, the deficiency of energy sends a signal to the brain with an urge to have another meal. Hence, diabetic people are constantly hungry, no matter how recently they have eaten.

- Increased thirst

Since glucose level in blood remains high in a diabetic body, it becomes necessary to remove the excess glucose, and this happens during urination. But this also leads to losing additional water from the body and makes a person thirsty than usual.

- Frequent Urination

Kidneys are used to remove excess glucose from the blood in the body. This led to a diabetic person urinates more frequently, especially at night.

- Feeling Tired

The abnormal level of glucose and insufficient deliverance of sugar into body cells cause tiredness and fatigue.

- Slow healing of wound

Blood vessels and nerves are damaged by high sugar level, and this impairs blood circulation. Hence, even a small wound or even a cut may take weeks to heal properly and this slow healing increases the risk of infection.

- Blurry Vision

Since high sugar level damages blood vessels, it also damages tiny vessels in the eyes. This can lead to blurry vision, and if not treated timely, the diabetic person may lose his vision permanently.

- Itching and Infections

Excess glucose is food for yeast, and it may cause harmful effects of yeast infection. Yeast infection needs a warm environment and moist places so look out the moist area on your skin, in mouth or armpit. The sign of yeast infection is itchiness, burning, soreness, and redness.

- Tingling or numbness in hands and feet

When body nerves are damaged due to excess glucose in the blood, this may lead to pain, numbness, or tingling in your tongue, lips, cheeks, arms, and feet. And, it can get worse if a diabetic person doesn't get his treatment for this condition.
Other signs of diabetes are weight gain, soft and dark skin under armpit or neck, and headaches.

Types of Diabetes

Type 1 diabetes

Type 1 diabetes occurs due to a fault in the immune system, which mistakenly targets beta cells in the pancreas and destroys them. As a result, less or no insulin cause change in blood glucose level, and body cells don't receive enough glucose for functioning. Although anyone can develop type 1 diabetes, it is commonly found in children and young adults. Symptoms: tiredness, frequent urination, weight loss, itchiness, and above-average thirst If anyone shows any of the above symptoms, he should visit a doctor and do some blood or urine tests to diagnose type 1 diabetes. The common treatment of the cause of type 1 diabetes, which is impairment of pancreases is done by injecting insulin that can be delivered into the body by using insulin pumps and pens. Moreover, it is also important to keep a check on the balance of insulin doses with food intake. Hence, along with healthy diet, indulging body into physical activity regularly also helps in maintaining blood glucose level and reduce the risks of complications that come with type 1 diabetes.

Type 2 diabetes

In type 2 diabetes, the body is unable to metabolize glucose that may occur due to ineffectiveness to use produced insulin or is unable to produce insulin. This results in high levels of glucose in the blood that may cause serious damage to body organs. Type 2 diabetes has become very common and found in children, teens, and young adults. Symptoms: Obesity, eating unhealthy and junk food, having a family history of type 2 diabetes, high blood pressure, high cholesterol level, smoking, lack of physical activity

Compare to type 1 diabetes, type 2 diabetes is a serious condition, and it requires the use of insulin and anti-diabetic injection to keep glucose level under control. Another simple and easy way to reverse type 2 diabetes is regular exercise and eating healthy low-carb and very low-calorie food.

Gestational diabetes

Gestational diabetes is the result of high glucose levels during pregnancy. It usually develops in the third trimester and disappears when the baby born. Gestational diabetes occurs due to hormonal changes in the second or third trimester. As the baby grows, the need for insulin also increases by two to three times. But if the body fails to produce enough insulin, a simple sugar (glucose) won't move into the cells and stays in the blood. This causes high sugar levels and leads to gestational diabetes.
Finding out that you have gestational diabetes during one of the happiest times of life is indeed overwhelming. And, you may think it's too late to find out diabetes, but you can still get treatment, and after making healthy changes in your life, you can lead a healthy and happy pregnancy without causing any harm to your body and baby.

Type 3 diabetes

Type 3 diabetes has been proposed for Alzheimer disease when the brain become insulin resistant. Therefore, people who have a high risk to develop type 2 diabetes also have an increased risk of Alzheimer's.

Risks of Type-2 Diabetes

Anyone can develop diabetes, but the chances get high depending on the genes and lifestyle. Gene means family history and age, and these factors cannot be changed, but you can lead a healthy lifestyle by eating nutritious food, doing physical activities and exercise, and monitoring your weight.

You have high chances to develop diabetes if you are

- Obese or overweight
- Age of 45 or above
- Have a high carb and fatty diet
- High alcohol intake
- Have close relatives suffering from diabetes
- Have a family history of gestational diabetes
- Have a family history of diabetes
- Have high blood pressure
- Have depression
- Have dark and velvety skin under armpits or neck
- Low level of good cholesterol (HDL)
- High level of bad cholesterol (triglycerides)
- Born with a weight of 9 pounds or more
- Belong to ethnic groups such as Asian Americans, Hispanic Americans, African American and Native American

The link between obesity and type 2 Diabetes

Being overweight or obese significantly increases the risk of high blood pressure, heart stroke, and diabetes. Obesity can occur due to many different reasons, including consuming high-calorie food, unhealthy lifestyle, and getting insufficient sleep.

But how being obese leads to the development of type 2 diabetes?

Type 2 diabetes is a condition in which blood glucose levels remain high. In an obese person, the fatty tissue in the body has to process more nutrients to perform its vital activities. For example, the heart of an obese person has to work hard than normal to pump blood throughout the body. Hence, this tress on tissues triggers inflammation which releases cytokine protein, which blocks the signal of the insulin receptor, resulting in cells becoming insulin resistant.

Insulin allows glucose, a simpler form of carbs, to be used by cells for energy. And, when cells become insulin resistant, they are unable to get sufficient amount of glucose, and the excess glucose in the blood leads to high blood glucose level or type 2 diabetes. This condition then triggers inflammation in cells that may lead to heart diseases.

Moreover, obesity triggers changes in metabolism, and as a result, it causes the release of fat molecules into the blood. The metabolic change affects insulin-responsive cells and decreases insulin sensitivity, which leads to type 2 diabetes.

How can diabetes be prevented and controlled

Following are some helpful tips to avoid obesity:

- Prevention of obesity in Kids:

Mothers are encouraged to breastfeed their kids as breastfeeding is associated with reducing the risks of obesity.

Growing kids don't need a huge amount of food. Therefore, keeping a check on their daily portion of food helps in preventing blood sugar level. This can be done by giving kids about 40 calories of food for every inch of their height.

Preventing diabetes is all about to develop healthy eating habits. Kids should be encouraged to try a variety of vegetables, fruits, and protein from an early age so that when they grow up, they can incorporate these foods into their own diet.

Overeating is one of the major causes of obesity because it is eating, even if you are not hungry. As a result, excess food is stored as fats in the body, and that leads to obesity. Make your children habitual to eat slowly and only when they are hungry.

Incorporate fun physical activities in the daily lifestyle of kids. Activities could be sports, gym or yoga class, games, and even outdoor chores.

Not getting enough sleep may lead to an increase in weight. Therefore, kids should develop healthy eating habits and make sure of this by making a sleeping schedule and sleeping on a soft mattress with a comfortable pillow.

- Prevention of obesity in Adults:

Maintaining your healthy eating routine plays a vital part in keeping away obesity. Therefore, eat less bad fat and more good fats such as low-carb foods that can improve your blood cholesterol level and reduce the risks of obesity.

Processed and sugary foods increase the risks of obesity. Processed foods are high in sugar and fats, which may encourage overeating, and that leads to obesity.

Dietary fiber plays a role in controlling obesity and helps in maintaining weight. Therefore, make vegetables and fruits, which are high in fiber, a major part of your meal.

Join a support group or include your family and friends in your journey to weight loss. Getting more people to involve will motivate you a lot and help you maintain your healthy lifestyle.

Incorporate aerobics and weight training activities in your lifestyle to lose weight. Start with moderate aerobic activity for 150 minutes per week and then switch to vigorous activities. Moreover, do weight training at least two times per week.

Last but not least, it gets so much easier to keep track of your weight loss if you cook your own food. You can create your food budget, purchase healthy foods from grocery shops, and prep meals on your own.

A healthy meal can help ease the effects of Diabetes

Eating healthy meals and doing a physical activity not only control the effect of diabetes, they can create a positive impact on overall health. To manage the effects of diabetes, you need to balance what you drink and eat with being active and taking diabetic medicines. Moreover, what you choose to eat, how much you eat and when you eat are all important in keeping your blood glucose level in check.

Indeed, making changes in your eating and drinking habits is challenging in the beginning, but once your body gets habitual with your new lifestyle, you can achieve your health goal in no time.

So being a person with diabetes doesn't mean that eating those foods that you don't enjoy. Not at all. The good news is that you can eat everything you love, but you have to consume small portions and less often. You can do this with the plate method. This method adds a variety of food in your plate and helps you control your portion sizes. For example, you can divide a plate into three portions, half of the plate for non-starchy veggies, the one-fourth portion for protein and the other one-fourth portion for grains, along with some fruits and a glass of low-fat milk.

Food to eat

The food you can eat in diabetes are:

Vegetables:	Some starchy vegetables including potatoes, peas, and corn
	All non-starchy vegetables such as bell peppers, tomatoes, broccoli, cauliflower, carrots, and leafy greens
Fruits:	All fruits that have low glycemic index including apples, bananas, berries, melon, grapes, oranges and avocado
Grains:	Wheat, rice, quinoa, barley, oats, cereal, cornmeal, whole wheat flour, pasta, tortillas
Protein:	Poultry such as chicken, turkey, and lamb, lean meat, meat substitutes such as tofu and tempeh, seafood, salmon, tuna and other fishes, eggs and dairy products such as low-fat milk, yogurt, and cheeses
Nuts:	Walnuts, peanuts, etc.
Dried beans:	Red beans, black beans, chickpeas, and split peas
Oils:	All oils that are liquid at room temperature, such as olive oil and canola oil
Beverages:	Unsweetened tea and coffee, plenty of water and a moderate amount of alcohol

Food to avoid

The foods and drinks that need to limit in diabetes are:

Vegetables:	All starchy vegetables except for those mentioned above.
Fruits:	All fruits that have a high glycemic index
Protein:	All high-fat dairy products

White sugar

Fried foods
Foods that are high in salt, trans fats, and saturated fats
Sweets such as candy, ice cream, and baked goods
Processed foods and snacks
Beverages that are sweetened such as processed juices, soda, and energy drink

Chapter2: Instant Pot Basic

The instant pot is the fastest-growing kitchen appliance in the culinary market. This multi-purpose pressure cooker has automated conventional pressure cooking and promotes hassle-free cooking. It's a blessing for individuals who despite being busy prefers home-cooked food and are health conscious. Instant pot totally simplifies exhaustive cooking; there is no need to stir food frequently, keep a check on cooking temperature, move food from one pan to another, and only one pot to wash. Now, there could not be any excuse to not prepare a home-cooked meal.

To name a few, instant pot saves time, retain food nutrients, and enhance its texture and taste. Let's check out how instant pot makes cooking so easy and simple.

Instant pot benefits

- The instant pot is one machine that does the job of seven. It is a frying/sautéing pan, simmering pot, steamer, warming pot, rice cooker, slow cooker, and yogurt maker. Yes, it is a jack of all trades, you can cook anything and everything in it.
- With so many built-in functions in the instant pot, one could imagine its operation's super complicated. No! All you need to do is dump your food into the inner pot, and press a few buttons and your food is good to go for cooking.
- The instant pot is an energy-efficient cooking appliance. It is evaluated that instant pot reduces energy and cooking time by 70 percent for frying, sautéing, boiling, baking, and steaming of food. It does this by using its inner pot, which is fully insulated, and this ensures that an instant pot doesn't exert too much energy for heating. Moreover, instant pot requires only less cooking liquid than other cooking methods, and thus, food is boiled faster in it.
- Boiling tends to diminish nutrients in food. However, boiling in instant pot is so faster and evenly, which allow foods to retain their nutrients.
- Cooking in open utensils expose food to heat and oxygen that diminished flavors and change texture. With the airtight cooking in the instant pot, the food retains its bright color and enable flavor to infuse in each other in record time, and more profoundly.
- Cooking is not something funny and nor pretty. And, on a hot day, cooking is much like working in a hot sauna bathroom. But not anymore! Now, you can walk away from food in instant pot and continue with your work. Moreover, it won't heat its surroundings, so there is no noise, no smell, and no heat while cooking with the instant pot.
- Instant pot can cook for everyone, be it an individual, couple, medium-size family and a crowd. It comes with all sizes, from 2 to 12 quarts, and range of cooking

options. And, the best part, it's also not heavy to move around in the kitchen.

The main functions

Manual Button:	The manual button is the most utilized button. It uses to set cooking time on the instant pot to whatever you like. Hit "Manual" when ready to use it, then hit "pressure" to select high/low pressure and then press "+ or –" to adjust the cooking time.
Pressure Button:	Use the pressure button to switch from high to low. Press "pressure" button after hitting the "manual" button and then press "+ or –" to set cooking time as needed.
Sauté/Simmer Button:	This button is used for frying or browning vegetables, meat, and thickening cooking sauce at the end of pressure cooking. Press the "Sauté" button, press "adjust" button and then "+ or –" to set cooking temperature. When instant pot displays "hot," add your ingredients into the pot and start browning. One sauté/simmer session last 30 minutes.
Delay Cooking /Timer Button:	This button is used to delay cooking time. Press "Manual" button or "Slow Cooker" button, press "+ or –" button to set cooking time, then hit "timer" button within 10 seconds and press "+ or –" button to set delay time as required.
Slow Cooker Button:	Slow cooker button switches instant pot to slow cook or keep warm mode, but the temperature settings are not equivalent. Press the slow cooker button and then hit the adjust button to set the heat setting. The low setting is equivalent to keep the warm setting on the regular slow cooker, the medium setting is like low heat setting on the regular slow cooker, and the high setting is like medium-high setting on the regular slow cooker.

Cleaning tips

Instant pot requires cleaning do prevent food residues, weird smells due to pressure cooking and clogging. Here are some cleaning steps which every instant pot owner should know.

1. Clean the main cooker and base

When you are ready to clean instant pot, unplug it and make no other contact with an electric source is there.

Take out the inner pot from its base. Then use a clean and damp towel to wipe clean the outside and inside of the main cooker and its base. Brush cooker with a pastry brush or paintbrush to remove all nook and crannies of the cooker and remove all the food debris from its bottom. Wipe clean with a dry cloth at the end.

2. Clean the lid and its small parts

Wash the lid with warm soapy water. Then Remove quick release handle and steam valve and wash them with warm soapy water to remove blocked food residues. Detach the condensation cup and wash it until clean or replace it.

Wash sealing ring in the lid. This prevents absorption of food colors and their odors by the rind. It is recommended to wash the sealing ring in the top rack of dishwasher. If you notice any crack or deformity in the ring, place the ring immediately.

If the sealing ring has taken any food smell, deodorize it by cleaning with giving it vinegar steam. For this, pour 1 cup water and 1 cup vinegar into the inner pot along with some lemon peels. Shut instant pot with lid and steam for 2 minutes, and do natural pressure release. Open the instant pot, remove the sealing ring, and let dry at room temperature.

3. Scrub the inner pot

Wash inner pot in dishwater but make sure it is dishwasher safe.

If there are any stains in the inner pot, soak the instant pot in vinegar for 5 minutes, then rinse it and wash with soapy water. To remove food stains from the inner pot, soak the pot in warm soapy water, then use a damp sponge to scrub away the food residue and rinse the inner pot.

Then use paper towels and vinegar to wipe clean it. This will return the shine of instant pot and remove detergent residues. Then Wipe clean the inside and outside of the inner pot with a wet kitchen cloth.

Wash steamer rack or trivet stand with warm soapy water and wipe clean with paper towels.

4. Wipe the outside of Instant Pot

Take a damp sponge or kitchen towels and use it to gently clean the outer body of the instant pot. Remove any stains with white vinegar followed by cleaning with a damp kitchen towel.

5. Reassemble Instant pot

Finally, put together all the pieces of the instant pot and reassemble it.

Chapter3: The Benefits of the Diabetes Instant Pot

The instant pot has made healthy cooking very easy than it was ever before. Using its terrific built-in functions and incredibly fast cooking, you can cook your food to meet your diet requirement.

So, is Instant pot beneficial for cooking diabetic-friendly foods?

Yes, it is.

Being a multi-purpose pressure cooker, you do a variety of cooking in one appliance. You can use it to slow cook your meats, sauté your veggies, boil your oats, simmer and pressure cook your soups, stews and other meals. Hence, there is no need to defrost food, prepping ingredients, cooking in multiple pots, and making a mess on stovetop anymore. Just plug in instant pot, press some buttons and let it do the cooking for you.

Read on to know how you can meal plan for 30 days.

Chapter4: 30-Day Meal Plan

Day 1

Breakfast: Egg and Vegetable Frittata

Lunch: Zucchini Soup

Dinner: Pea and Cottage Cheese Curry

Dessert: Chocolate Fudge

Day 2

Breakfast: Apple Pie Oatmeal

Lunch: Yellow Lentils

Dinner: Irish Beef Stew

Dessert: Carrot Cake

Day 3

Breakfast: Mexican Breakfast Scramble

Lunch: Vegetable Lentil Soup

Dinner: Chicken Tortilla Soup

Dessert: Lime Curd

Day 4

Breakfast: Carrot Muffins

Lunch: Mac and Cheese

Dinner: Chicken, Pasta and Spinach Soup

Dessert: Oatmeal Bites

Day 5

Breakfast: Triple-Grain Flapjacks

Lunch: Couscous Tomatoes

Dinner: Chili Lime Salmon

Dessert: Chocolate Pudding

Day 6

Breakfast: Granola

Lunch: Collard Greens

Dinner: Turkey Chili

Dessert: Poached Spiced Pears

Day 7

Breakfast: English Muffins

Lunch: Spiced Tomato Lentil Soup

Dinner: Roast Vegetable and Bean Stew

Dessert: Carrot Cake

Day 8

Breakfast: Banana Pancakes

Lunch: Turkey Burger Patty

Dinner: Lentils with Lamb

Dessert: Apple and Cinnamon Cake

Day 9

Breakfast: Tomato Basil Frittata

Lunch: Barley Pilaf with Tofu

Dinner: Beef and Rice Stuffed Bell Peppers

Dessert: Brownies

Day 10

Breakfast: Triple-Grain Flapjacks

Lunch: Rutabaga Stew

Dinner: Beef Stroganoff

Dessert: Oatmeal Bites

Day 11

Breakfast: Carrot Muffins

Lunch: Chickpea Salad

Dinner: Rosemary Leg of Lamb

Dessert: Lime Curd

Day 12

Breakfast: Apple Pie Oatmeal

Lunch: Pinto Beans

Dinner: Chili Lime Steak Bowl

Dessert: Carrot Cake

Day 13

Breakfast: Mexican Breakfast Scramble

Lunch: Butternut Squash and Carrot Soup

Dinner: Pork Roast

Dessert: Chocolate Pudding

Day 14

Breakfast: Hard-Boiled Eggs

Lunch: Split Pea Soup

Dinner: Beef Goulash

Dessert: Poached Spiced Pears

Day 15

Breakfast: Granola

Lunch: Tuna Melt

Dinner: Pesto Chicken and Green Beans

Dessert: Brownies

Day 16

Breakfast: English Muffins

Lunch: Seasoned Beans, Rice, and Vegetables

Dinner: Mediterranean Stew

Dessert: Chocolate Fudge

Day 17

Breakfast: Triple-Grain Flapjacks

Lunch: Black Beans, Corn, and Cheese on Sweet Potato

Dinner: Chicken & Rice

Dessert: Lime Curd

Day 18

Breakfast: Egg and Vegetable Frittata

Lunch: Black Beans, Corn, and Cheese on Sweet Potato

Dinner: Beef Fajitas

Dessert: Carrot Cake

Day 19

Breakfast: Carrot Muffins

Lunch: Barley and Wild Mushroom Risotto

Dinner: Garlic Herb Chicken

Dessert: Oatmeal Bites

Day 20

Breakfast: Apple Pie Oatmeal

Lunch: Chicken Tortilla Soup

Dinner: Black and Pinto Bean Chili

Dessert: Chocolate Pudding

Day 21

Breakfast: Hard-Boiled Eggs

Lunch: Spinach Stuffed Chicken Breast

Dinner: Balsamic Beef Pot Roast

Dessert: Apple and Cinnamon Cake

Day 22

Breakfast: Tomato Basil Frittata

Lunch: Clam Chowder

Dinner: Chicken Pea Curry

Dessert: Lime Curd

Day 23

Breakfast: Mexican Breakfast Scramble

Lunch: Wheat Berry, Black Bean, and Avocado Salad

Dinner: Pork Chops

Dessert: Poached Spiced Pears

Day 24

Breakfast: Banana Pancakes

Lunch: Chicken Stuffed Potatoes

Dinner: Barley Pilaf with Tofu

Dessert: Chocolate Fudge

Day 25

Breakfast: Apple Pie Oatmeal

Lunch: Vegetable Lentil Soup

Dinner: Spiced Tomato Lentil Soup

Dessert: Brownies

Day 26

Breakfast: Triple-Grain Flapjacks

Lunch: Chicken Tacos

Dinner: Pea and Cottage Cheese Curry

Dessert: Chocolate Pudding

Day 27

Breakfast: Hard-Boiled Eggs

Lunch: Pork Carnitas

Dinner: Cauliflower Fried Rice

Dessert: Oatmeal Bites

Day 28

Breakfast: Granola

Lunch: Irish Beef Stew

Dinner: Rutabaga Stew

Dessert: Carrot Cake

Day 29

Breakfast: Carrot Muffins

Lunch: Pesto Chicken and Green Beans

Dinner: Lamb Steaks

Dessert: Lime Curd

Day 30

Breakfast: English Muffins

Lunch: Baked Butternut Squash

Dinner: Mustard Pork Chops

Dessert: Apple and Cinnamon Cake

Chapter5: Breakfast

Egg and Vegetable Frittata

Servings: 4
Preparation time: 10 minutes
Cooking time: 15 minutes

Nutrition Value:

Calories: 200 Cal, Carbs: 15 g, Fat: 8 g, Protein: 16 g, Fiber: 3 g.

Ingredients:

- 1 1/3 cups corn kernels, frozen
- 1 cup finely chopped green onion
- 1 cup chopped kale
- 1 cup chopped red bell pepper
- 1/4 teaspoon and 1/8 teaspoon salt, divided
- 1/4 teaspoon dried thyme
- 4 eggs
- 4 egg whites
- 2-ounce grated cheddar cheese
- 1 cup water

Method:

1. Take four ramekins, grease with cooking spray and then evenly fill them with corn, pepper, kale and green onion and press down slightly.
2. Crack eggs in a bowl, add egg whites, ¼ teaspoon salt, thyme, then whisk until combined and pour this mixture evenly over vegetables in ramekins.
3. Cut out four pieces of aluminum foil, about 6-inch, grease one side with oil and cover each ramekin with a piece of foil, coated side down.
4. Plugin instant pot, insert the inner pot, pour in water, then insert trivet stand and stack ramekins on it.
5. Shut the instant pot with its lid and turn the pressure knob to seal the pot.
6. Press the 'manual' button, then press the 'timer' to set the cooking time to 10 minutes and cook at high pressure, instant pot will take 5 minutes or more for building its inner pressure.

7. When the timer beeps, press 'cancel' button and do quick pressure release until pressure nob drops down.
8. Remove ramekins from the instant pot, uncover them and then sprinkle cheese and remaining salt.
9. Let ramekins stand for 5 minutes and then serve.

Apple Pie Oatmeal

Servings: 4
Preparation time: 15 minutes
Cooking time: 10 minutes

Nutrition Value:

Calories: 171 Cal, Carbs: 32.6 g, Fat: 2.6 g, Protein: 5.1 g, Fiber: 5.3 g.

Ingredients:

- 1/2 cup oats, steel-cut
- ½ of a medium apple, peeled and chopped
- 1/8 teaspoon salt
- ¼ teaspoon apple pie spice
- 1 cup apple juice, unsweetened
- 1 1/2 cups milk, unsweetened and fat-free
- ½ cup Greek yogurt, fat-free

Method:

1. Plugin instant pot, insert the inner pot, add all the ingredients except for milk and yogurt and stir until mixed.
2. Shut the instant pot with its lid and turn the pressure knob to seal the pot.
3. Press the 'manual' button, then press the 'timer' to set the cooking time to 5 minutes and cook at high pressure, instant pot will take 5 minutes or more for building its inner pressure.
4. When the timer beeps, press 'cancel' button and do natural pressure release for 10 minutes and then do quick pressure release until pressure nob drops down.
5. Open the instant pot, add milk and yogurt, stir well and serve.

Mexican Breakfast Scramble

Servings: 4
Preparation time: 5 minutes
Cooking time: 8 minutes

Nutrition Value:

Calories: 227 Cal, Carbs: 22 g, Fat: 5 g, Protein: 24 g, Fiber: 3 g.

Ingredients:

- 6-ounce cooked chicken sausages, sliced
- 1 cup diced red bell pepper
- 1 jalapeño chili pepper, seeded and chopped
- 1 medium onion, peeled and sliced
- 4 corn tortillas, about 6 inches
- ⅛ teaspoon salt
- 1 tablespoon olive oil
- 8 eggs, beaten
- ¼ cup crumbled queso fresco

Method:

1. Set oven t0 400 degrees F and let preheat.
2. Then place tortillas on a baking sheet, place it in the oven and bake for 8 to 10 minutes or until tortillas are crispy.
3. When done, break tortilla into small pieces and set aside.
4. Plugin instant pot, insert the inner pot, press sauté/simmer button and when hot, add oil and sausage, bell pepper, chili pepper, and onion and cook for 5 minutes or more until vegetables are softened.
5. Season vegetables with salt, add tortilla pieces along with queso fresco, then pour in the egg mixture and cook for 3 to 4 minutes or until the bottom of the mixture begin to set, don't stir.
6. Fold the cooked egg side to flow uncooked egg mixture underneath it and continue cooking for 2 to 3 minutes or until the egg is cooked through but also moist.
7. Press the cancel button and slide the egg onto a plate.
8. Serve straight away.

Triple-Grain Flapjacks

Servings: 16
Preparation time: 15 minutes
Cooking time: 30 minutes

Nutrition Value:
Calories: 220 Cal, Carbs: 35 g, Fat: 6 g, Protein: 7 g, Fiber: 2 g.

Ingredients:

- ½ cup dried blueberries
- 1½ cups all-purpose flour
- ½ cup rolled oats
- ½ cup cornmeal
- ½ teaspoon salt
- 3 tablespoons brown sugar
- 2½ teaspoons baking powder
- 3 tablespoons olive oil
- 1 egg
- 1¾ cups milk, fat-free
- ¼ cup yogurt, low-fat
- Pineapple chunks for serving

Method:

1. Place flour in a large bowl, add cornmeal, salt, and baking powder and stir until well mixed.
2. Place oats in a food processor, add brown sugar and pulse for 1 to 2 minutes or until ground.
3. Tip the oat mixture into the bowl containing flour mixture and stir well.
4. Whisk together oil, egg, milk, and yogurt until smooth, then make a well in the center of the bowl containing flour mixture and pour egg mixture in it.
5. Stir the mixture until moist and thin batter comes together and then let it stand for 10 minutes or until slightly thick.
6. Then plug in instant pot, insert the inner pot, press sauté/simmer button and add oil and wait until hot.
7. Fold berries into the prepared batter, then pour in a ¼ cup of the batter into the instant pot and cook for 2 minutes per side or until nicely golden brown and cooked through.
8. When done, transfer pancake to a plate and use the remaining batter for cooking more pancakes.
9. Serve pancakes with pineapple chunks.

Banana Pancakes

Servings: 2
Preparation time: 5 minutes
Cooking time: 15 minutes

Nutrition Value:

Calories: 124 Cal, Carbs: 14 g, Fat: 5 g, Protein: 7 g, Fiber: 2 g.

Ingredients:

- 1 medium banana, peeled
- 2 eggs

Method:

1. Place banana in a food processor, add eggs and pulse for 1 minute or until smooth batter comes together.
2. Plugin instant pot, insert the inner pot, press sauté/simmer button, add oil and when hot, add 2 tablespoons of prepared batter for each pancake.
3. Cook pancakes for 2 minutes per side or until nicely golden brown and cooked through and when done, transfer pancakes to a plate.
4. Use remaining batter for cooking more pancakes and serve straightaway.

Tomato Basil Frittata

Servings: 8
Preparation time: 5 minutes
Cooking time: 25 minutes

Nutrition Value:

Calories: 129 Cal, Carbs: 2 g, Fat: 8 g, Protein: 11 g, Fiber: 1.4 g.

Ingredients:

- 1 cup frozen spinach, thawed
- 1 sliced tomato
- 1 diced tomato
- 2 cups thawed hash browns
- ¼ teaspoon ground black pepper
- 2 teaspoons dried basil
- 6 eggs
- ¼ cup milk, non-fat
- ½ cup cheddar cheese, low-fat
- 1 ½ cups water

Method:

1. Crack eggs in a bowl, add all the ingredients except for slice tomato and water and stir until combined.
2. Take a heatproof dish that fits into the instant pot, grease it with oil, then pour in the prepared batter and scatter sliced tomato on top.
3. Plugin instant pot, insert the inner pot, pour in water, then insert trivet stand and place dish on it.
4. Shut the instant pot with its lid and turn the pressure knob to seal the pot.
5. Press the 'manual' button, then press the 'timer' to set the cooking time to 20 minutes and cook at high pressure, instant pot will take 5 minutes or more for building its inner pressure.
6. When the timer beeps, press 'cancel' button and do quick pressure release until pressure nob drops down.
7. Open the instant pot, remove the dish from the instant pot, wipe any moisture from the top of frittata using paper towels, and serve.

Carrot Muffins

Servings: 6
Preparation time: 10 minutes
Cooking time: 20 minutes
Nutrition Value:
Calories: 251 Cal, Carbs: 41 g, Fat: 7 g, Protein: 4 g, Fiber: 3 g.
Ingredients:

- ¾ cup whole wheat flour
- ½ cup grated carrot
- 1/8 teaspoon salt
- ½ teaspoon ground cinnamon
- ½ teaspoon baking powder
- ½ teaspoon baking soda
- ¼ cup chocolate chips
- ¼ cup maple syrup
- ½ teaspoon vanilla extract, unsweetened
- ¼ cup avocado oil
- 2 tablespoons Greek yogurt
- 1 egg
- 1 ½ cup water

Method:

1. Place flour and carrot in a large bowl, add salt, cinnamon, baking powder, and baking soda and stir until mixed.
2. Crack an egg in another bowl, add remaining ingredients except for water and whisk until combined.
3. Stir flour mixture into the egg mixture, 4 tablespoons at a time, until smooth batter comes together and then evenly divide the mixture into six egg molds or silicone muffin cups.
4. Plugin instant pot, insert the inner pot, pour in water, then insert trivet stand and place muffin cups on it.
5. Shut the instant pot with its lid and turn the pressure knob to seal the pot.
6. Press the 'manual' button, then press the 'timer' to set the cooking time to 10 minutes and cook at high pressure, instant pot will take 5 minutes or more for building its inner pressure.
7. When the timer beeps, press 'cancel' button and do natural pressure release for 5 minutes and then do quick pressure release until pressure nob drops down.
8. Take out muffins from their cups and let cool for 10 minutes on a wire rack before serving.

Granola

Servings: 8
Preparation time: 5 minutes
Cooking time: 2 hours and 30 minutes

Nutrition Value:

Calories: 495 Cal, Carbs: 63 g, Fat: 25 g, Protein: 9 g, Fiber: 7 g.

Ingredients:

- 1/2 cup dried cranberries
- 4 cups rolled oats
- 1 cup roasted almonds, chopped
- 1/2 teaspoon salt
- 1/4 cup brown sugar
- 1/2 teaspoon cinnamon
- 1/2 cup honey
- 1 teaspoon vanilla extract, unsweetened
- 1/2 cup olive oil

Method:

1. Plugin instant pot, insert the inner pot, spray with oil, then add oats and almonds, sprinkle with salt, sugar, and cinnamon and stir until mixed.
2. Place honey in a small bowl, add vanilla and oil and whisk until combined.
3. Pour this mixture over oat mixture and stir until well combined.
4. Cover instant pot partly with a glass lid, then press the 'slow cook button, press the 'timer' to set the cooking time to 2 hours and 30 minutes at low heat setting, stirring granola mixture every 30 minutes.
5. When the timer beeps, press 'cancel' button and fold berries into the granola.
6. Spoon granola mixture onto a cookie sheet, spread it evenly and let cool.
7. Serve straight away or store granola into an airtight container for a week.

English Muffins

Servings: 4
Preparation time: 10 minutes
Cooking time: 25 minutes

Nutrition Value:

Calories: 170 Cal, Carbs: 3.4 g, Fat: 14.8 g, Protein: 6.1 g, Fiber: 1.3 g.

Ingredients:

- 2 tablespoons coconut flour
- ¼ teaspoon onion powder
- ¼ teaspoon garlic powder
- ½ teaspoon baking powder
- ⅛ teaspoon salt
- ¼ teaspoon Italian herb mix
- 2 tablespoons unsalted butter, softened
- 2 tablespoons grated Parmesan cheese
- 2-ounce cream cheese, softened
- 2 eggs
- 1 ½ cup water

Method:

1. Crack eggs in a bowl, add butter and cream cheese and beat until combined.
2. Then beat in flour, onion powder, garlic powder, baking powder, salt, and Italian herb mix until incorporated.
3. Take two pyrex glass container, grease with avocado, then evenly divide the prepared batter and then cover the container with aluminum foil.
4. Plugin instant pot, insert the inner pot, pour in water, insert trivet stand, and place containers on it.
5. Shut the instant pot with its lid and turn the pressure knob to seal the pot.
6. Press the 'manual' button, then press the 'timer' to set the cooking time to 20 minutes and cook at high pressure, instant pot will take 5 minutes or more for building its inner pressure.
7. When the timer beeps, press 'cancel' button and do quick pressure release until pressure nob drops down.
8. Open the instant pot, carefully remove containers, uncover them, and let cool completely.

9. Then take out muffin from each container, cut in half and toast each muffin slice until nicely golden brown.
10. Serve straight away.

Hard Boiled Eggs

Servings: 6
Preparation time: 5 minutes
Cooking time: 15 minutes

Nutrition Value:

Calories: 62 Cal, Carbs: 0 g, Fat: 4 g, Protein: 5 g, Fiber: 0 g.

Ingredients:

- 6 eggs
- 1 cup water

Method:

1. Plugin instant pot, insert the inner pot, pour in water, then insert steamer rack and place eggs on it.
2. Shut the instant pot with its lid and turn the pressure knob to seal the pot.
3. Press the 'manual' button, then press the 'timer' to set the cooking time to 5 minutes and cook at high pressure, instant pot will take 5 minutes or more for building its inner pressure.
4. When the timer beeps, press 'cancel' button and do natural pressure release for 5 minutes and then do quick pressure release until pressure nob drops down.
5. Open the instant pot, then transfer the boiled eggs into a bowl containing icy chilled water and let soak for 10 minutes.
6. Then crack the eggs and remove their shell.
7. Cut eggs into half, season with salt and cracked black pepper to taste and serve.

Chapter6: Soups and Stews

Spiced Tomato Lentil Soup

Servings: 8
Preparation time: 5 minutes
Cooking time: 25 minutes

Nutrition Value:

Calories: 156 Cal, Carbs: 27 g, Fat: 2 g, Protein: 8 g, Fiber: 6 g.

Ingredients:

- 1 cup yellow lentils
- 3 medium carrots, peeled and chopped
- 3 celery stalks, chopped
- 28-ounce crushed tomatoes, no salt added
- 1 medium white onion, peeled and chopped
- 1 tablespoon minced garlic
- ½ teaspoon salt
- ¼ teaspoon ground black pepper
- 1 tablespoon ground cumin
- 1 bay leaf
- 1 tablespoon olive oil
- 1 tablespoon tomato paste
- 4 cups vegetable broth
- 2 cups water

Method:

1. Plugin instant pot, insert the inner pot, press sauté/simmer button, add oil and when hot, add chopped carrots, celery, onion, and garlic and cook for 2 minutes or until fragrant.
2. Press the cancel button, add remaining ingredients, stir well, then shut the instant pot with its lid and turn the pressure knob to seal the pot.
3. Press the 'beans/chili' button, then press the 'timer' to set the cooking time to 15 minutes and cook at high pressure, instant pot will take 5 minutes or more for building its inner pressure.

4. When the timer beeps, press 'cancel' button and do quick pressure release until pressure nob drops down.
5. Open the instant pot and puree lentils with an immersion blender until smooth.
6. Ladle soup into bowls and serve.

Vegetable Lentil Soup

Servings: 10
Preparation time: 5 minutes
Cooking time: 6 hours

Nutrition Value:

Calories: 48.2 Cal, Carbs: 8.9 g, Fat: 0.2 g, Protein: 3.3 g, Fiber: 2.6 g.

Ingredients:

- 1/4 cup soy protein
- 1/2 cup dried lentils, rinsed
- 1 large potato, peeled and diced
- 1 cup chopped carrots
- 1/2 cups diced green beans
- 1 cup chopped zucchini
- 1 medium tomato, chopped
- 1/2 cup diced white onion
- 1 teaspoon minced garlic
- 1 teaspoon salt
- 1/4 teaspoon ground black pepper
- 2 basil leaves
- 1/4 cup tomato sauce
- 4 cups vegetable stock

Method:

1. Plugin instant pot, insert the inner pot, add all the ingredients, and stir until mixed.
2. Shut the instant pot with its lid and turn the pressure knob to seal the pot.
3. Press the 'slow cook' button, then press the 'timer' to set the cooking time to 6 hours at low heat setting.
4. When the timer beeps, press 'cancel' button and do natural pressure release for 10 minutes and then do quick pressure release until pressure nob drops down.
5. Open the instant pot, then ladle soup into bowls and serve.

Split Pea Soup

Servings: 8
Preparation time: 20 minutes
Cooking time: 28 minutes

Nutrition Value:

Calories: 122.7 Cal, Carbs: 15 g, Fat: 4 g, Protein: 11.8 g, Fiber: 5.2 g.

Ingredients:

- 1-pound green split peas, rinsed
- 1 medium white onion, peeled and diced
- 3 medium carrots, peeled and chopped
- 3 stalks of celery, diced
- 2 teaspoons minced garlic
- 1/2 teaspoon salt
- 1/4 teaspoon ground black pepper
- 2 bay leaves
- 1/4 teaspoon dried thyme
- 2 tablespoons olive oil
- 6 cups vegetable broth

Method:

1. Plugin instant pot, insert the inner pot, press sauté/simmer button, add oil and when hot, add onion and celery along with thyme and bay leaves.
2. Cook for 5 minutes or until onion begins to tender, then remaining ingredients and stir until mixed.
3. Press the cancel button, shut the instant pot with its lid and turn the pressure knob to seal the pot.
4. Press the 'manual' button, then press the 'timer' to set the cooking time to 18 minutes and cook at high pressure, instant pot will take 5 minutes or more for building its inner pressure.
5. When the timer beeps, press 'cancel' button and do natural pressure release for 10 minutes and then do quick pressure release until pressure nob drops down.
6. Open the instant pot, remove and discard bay leaves and ladle soup into bowls.
7. Serve straight away.

Chicken Tortilla Soup

Servings: 4
Preparation time: 5 minutes
Cooking time: 6 hours

Nutrition Value:

Calories: 212 Cal, Carbs: 17 g, Fat: 5 g, Protein: 23 g, Fiber: 1 g.

Ingredients:

- 2 cups cooked chicken, shredded
- 2 cups mixed vegetables, stir-fry
- 14.5-ounce stewed tomatoes, Mexican-style
- 1 teaspoon minced garlic
- 2½ cups water
- 1 cup chicken broth
- 1 cup bag tortilla chips
- 1 jalapeño chili peppers, sliced

Method:

1. Plugin instant pot, insert the inner pot, add all the ingredients except for chips and stir until mixed.
2. Shut the instant pot with its lid and turn the pressure knob to seal the pot.
3. Press the 'slow cook' button, then press the 'timer' to set the cooking time to 6 hours at low heat setting.
4. When the timer beeps, press 'cancel' button and do natural pressure release for 10 minutes and then do quick pressure release until pressure nob drops down.
5. Open the instant pot, ladle soup into bowls, top with tortilla chips and serve.

Butternut Squash and Carrot Soup

Servings: 6
Preparation time: 5 minutes
Cooking time: 20 minutes

Nutrition Value:

Calories: 166 Cal, Carbs: 19 g, Fat: 10 g, Protein: 2 g, Fiber: 3 g.

Ingredients:

- 1 medium butternut squash, peeled & cubed
- 3 medium carrots, peeled & chopped
- 1 medium white onion, peeled and diced
- 1 teaspoon minced garlic
- 1 tablespoon grated ginger
- 2 cups vegetable broth
- 1 tablespoon curry powder
- 1/2 teaspoon garam masala
- 1/4 teaspoon turmeric powder
- 1 teaspoon salt
- 1/4 teaspoon cayenne
- 1 lime, juiced

Method:

1. Plugin instant pot, insert the inner pot, add all the ingredients, and stir until mixed.
2. Shut the instant pot with its lid and turn the pressure knob to seal the pot.
3. Press the 'manual' button, then press the 'timer' to set the cooking time to 15 minutes and cook at high pressure, instant pot will take 5 minutes or more for building its inner pressure.
4. When the timer beeps, press 'cancel' button and do quick pressure release until pressure nob drops down.
5. Open the instant pot, stir the soup and ladle into serving bowls.
6. Drizzle soup with lime juice and serve.

Irish Beef Stew

Servings: 4
Preparation time: 20 minutes
Cooking time: 35 minutes

Nutrition Value:

Calories: 392.8 Cal, Carbs: 61.6 g, Fat: 4.1 g, Protein: 29.1 g, Fiber: 9.8 g.

Ingredients:

- 1-pound beef, cut into 1-inch pieces
- 1 large white onion, peeled and diced
- 2 stalks of celery, sliced
- 2 medium potatoes, cut into 1-inch pieces
- 2 medium carrots, peeled and sliced
- 1 teaspoon minced garlic
- 1 teaspoon salt
- 1/2 teaspoon ground black pepper
- 1 teaspoon dried thyme
- 1 tablespoon dried parsley
- 1 bay leaf
- 1 tablespoon olive oil
- 1 cup beef stock
- 2 tablespoons cornstarch
- 2 tablespoons warm water

Method:

1. Plugin instant pot, insert the inner pot, press sauté/simmer button, add oil and when hot, add onion, celery, carrot, and garlic and cook for 5 minutes or until softened.
2. Add remaining ingredients, except for cornstarch and warm water, stir until mixed and press the cancel button.
3. Shut the instant pot with its lid, turn the pressure knob to seal the pot, press the 'manual' button, then press the 'timer' to set the cooking time to 20 minutes and cook at high pressure, instant pot will take 5 minutes or more for building its inner pressure.

4. When the timer beeps, press 'cancel' button and do natural pressure release for 10 minutes and then do quick pressure release until pressure nob drops down.
5. Open the instant pot, stir together cornstarch and water, add into the stew, stir well and let stew rest for 5 minutes or until slightly thick.
6. Ladle stew into the bowls and serve.

Zucchini Soup

Servings: 2
Preparation time: 5 minutes
Cooking time: 12 minutes

Nutrition Value:

Calories: 141 Cal, Carbs: 7 g, Fat: 11 g, Protein: 3.5 g, Fiber: 3 g.

Ingredients:

- 2 medium zucchinis, chopped
- 1/2 teaspoon onion powder
- 1/2 teaspoon garlic powder
- 1/2 teaspoon salt
- 1/4 teaspoon ground black pepper
- 1/2 teaspoon curry powder
- 1 cup coconut milk, reduced-fat and unsweetened
- 1 cup of water

Method:

1. Plugin instant pot, insert the inner pot, pour in water, then insert steamer basket and place zucchini pies on it.
2. Shut the instant pot with its lid and turn the pressure knob to seal the pot.
3. Press the 'steam' button, then press the 'timer' to set the cooking time to 2 minutes and cook at high pressure, instant pot will take 5 minutes or more for building its inner pressure.
4. When the timer beeps, press 'cancel' button and do natural pressure release for 5 minutes and then do quick pressure release until pressure nob drops down.
5. Open the instant pot, transfer zucchini to a plate to cool for 5 minutes, then place zucchini pieces in a food processor and add remaining ingredients.
6. Pulse zucchini for 1 to 2 minutes or until smooth and then evenly divide between bowls.
7. Serve straight away.

Rutabaga Stew

Servings: 6
Preparation time: 5 minutes
Cooking time: 25 minutes

Nutrition Value:

Calories: 85.3 Cal, Carbs: 12.9 g, Fat: 2.1 g, Protein: 3.7 g, Fiber: 3.9 g.

Ingredients:

- 2 medium rutabagas, peeled and diced
- 1 stalk of celery, diced
- 2 medium beets, peeled and diced
- 2 medium carrots, peeled and diced
- ½ of small red onion, peeled and diced
- 1 teaspoon salt
- 1/3 teaspoon ground black pepper
- 1 1/4 teaspoons olive oil
- 2 ½ cups chicken stock

Method:

1. Plugin instant pot, insert the inner pot, press sauté/simmer button, add oil and when hot, add celery, onion, and garlic and cook for 5 minutes or until tender.
2. Add remaining ingredients, stir until mixed, then press the cancel button, shut the instant pot with its lid and turn the pressure knob to seal the pot.
3. Press the 'manual' button, then press the 'timer' to set the cooking time to 15 minutes and cook at high pressure, instant pot will take 5 minutes or more for building its inner pressure.
4. When the timer beeps, press 'cancel' button and do quick pressure release until pressure nob drops down.
5. Open the instant pot, stir the soup and then puree using an immersion blender until smooth.
6. Ladle soup into bowls and serve.

Clam Chowder

Servings: 8
Preparation time: 5 minutes
Cooking time: 10 minutes

Nutrition Value:

Calories: 82 Cal, Carbs: 15.8 g, Fat: 0.2 g, Protein: 3.9 g, Fiber: 2.1 g.

Ingredients:

- 2 cups chopped clams
- 2 medium potatoes, peeled and chopped
- 1 cup chopped green bell pepper
- 14.5-ounce diced tomatoes
- 1/4 cup chopped green onions
- 1 teaspoon salt
- 1/4 teaspoon ground black pepper
- 1 cup tomato and clam juice cocktail
- ½ cup water

Method:

1. Plugin instant pot, insert the inner pot, add all the ingredients, and stir until mixed.
2. Shut the instant pot with its lid, turn the pressure knob to seal the pot, press the 'manual' button, then press the 'timer' to set the cooking time to 5 minutes and cook at high pressure, instant pot will take 5 minutes or more for building its inner pressure.
3. When the timer beeps, press 'cancel' button and do quick pressure release until pressure nob drops down.
4. Open the instant pot and stir the chowder, if the chowder is thin then press the 'sauté/simmer' button and cook soup until it reaches to desired thickness.
5. Ladle chowder into bowls and serve.

Mediterranean Stew

Servings: 5
Preparation time: 5 minutes
Cooking time: 10 hours

Nutrition Value:

Calories: 122 Cal, Carbs: 30.5 g, Fat: 0.5 g, Protein: 3.4 g, Fiber: 8 g.

Ingredients:

- 1/2 of medium butternut squash, peeled, seeded, and cubed
- 1 cup cubed eggplant
- 1 cup cubed zucchini
- 5-ounce okra
- 1/2 of medium carrot, peeled and sliced
- 1/2 of medium tomato, chopped
- 1/2 cup chopped white onion
- ½ teaspoon minced garlic
- 1 teaspoon salt
- 1/8 teaspoon paprika
- 1/8 teaspoon crushed red pepper
- 1/8 teaspoon ground turmeric
- 1/4 teaspoon ground cumin
- 2 tablespoons raisins
- 4-ounce tomato sauce
- ½ cup vegetable broth

Method:

1. Plugin instant pot, insert the inner pot, add all the ingredients, and stir until mixed.
2. Press the cancel button, shut the instant pot with its lid and turn the pressure knob to seal the pot.
3. Press the 'slow cook' button, then press the 'timer' to set the cooking time to 10 hours at low heat setting.
4. When the timer beeps, press 'cancel' button and do natural pressure release for until pressure nob drops down.
5. Open the instant pot, then ladle stew into bowls and serve.

Chapter7: Meatless Mains

Couscous Tomatoes

Servings: 8
Preparation time: 20 minutes
Cooking time: 18 minutes

Nutrition Value:

Calories: 175 Cal, Carbs: 28 g, Fat: 6 g, Protein: 5 g, Fiber: 5 g.

Ingredients:

- 1/2 cup couscous, uncooked
- 8 large tomatoes
- 1 small eggplant, diced into 1/2-inch pieces
- 1/2 cup dried apricots, chopped
- 1/2 cup almonds, sliced
- 1 ½ teaspoon salt
- ¾ teaspoon ground black pepper
- ½ teaspoon ground cumin
- 1 teaspoon ground coriander
- 1/8 teaspoon ground cinnamon
- 2 tablespoons chopped mint
- 1 tablespoon olive oil, divided
- 1 teaspoon harissa paste
- 1 cup vegetable broth

Method:

1. Cut off tomato from the top, then scoop out the seeds and sprinkle the hollow inside with some salt.
2. Then place tomatoes onto a paper towel-lined plate and set aside until tomatoes are drained.
3. Meanwhile, plug-in instant pot, insert the inner pot, press sauté/simmer button and when hot, add ½ tablespoon oil and almonds and cook for 2 to 4 minutes or until nicely golden brown.
4. Transfer almonds to a plate and set aside, then add remaining oil along with eggplant pieces and cook for 5 minutes or until nicely browned on all sides.

5. Season eggplant with cinnamon, cumin, coriander, then cook for 30 seconds or until fragrant, add couscous and stir well.
6. Press the cancel button, pour in the broth, then shut the instant pot with its lid and turn the pressure knob to seal the pot.
7. Press the 'manual' button, then press the 'timer' to set the cooking time to 2 minutes and cook at high pressure, instant pot will take 5 minutes or more for building its inner pressure.
8. When the timer beeps, press 'cancel' button and do natural pressure release for 10 minutes or until pressure nob drops down.
9. Open the instant pot, then fluff couscous with a fork, add apricots, cooked almonds and mint and stir until combined.
10. Pour harissa paste over couscous, season with salt and black pepper and spoon the mixture into hollowed tomatoes.
11. Serve immediately.

Barley Pilaf with Tofu

Servings: 4
Preparation time: 10 minutes
Cooking time: 30 minutes

Nutrition Value:

Calories: 571 Cal, Carbs: 77 g, Fat: 15 g, Protein: 23.6 g, Fiber: 18 g.

Ingredients:

- 4-ounce pearl barley, uncooked
- ¼ teaspoon white pepper
- 1 teaspoon ground cumin
- 1 teaspoon ground cinnamon
- 1 ¾ cup vegetable broth
- 4 teaspoons olive oil
- 6-ounce firm tofu, drained and sliced
- 1 teaspoon minced garlic
- 1 teaspoon grated ginger
- 1/2 teaspoon Chinese five-spice mix
- 1 tablespoon chopped coriander
- 1 medium red onion, peeled and sliced
- 1 medium zucchini, diced
- 1 medium red bell pepper, chopped
- 1 medium yellow bell pepper, finely chopped
- 4-ounce frozen peas, defrosted
- 2 teaspoons soy sauce
- 3-ounce pomegranate seeds

Method:

1. Plugin instant pot, insert the inner pot, add barley, stir in white pepper, cumin, and cinnamon, and then pour in broth.
2. Shut the instant pot with its lid and turn the pressure knob to seal the pot.
3. Press the 'manual' button, then press the 'timer' to set the cooking time to 20 minutes and cook at high pressure, instant pot will take 5 minutes or more for building its inner pressure.

4. Meanwhile, place a skillet pan over medium heat, add 2 teaspoons oil and when hot, add tofu slices and cook for 5 to 7 minutes or until nicely browned on all sides.
5. When done, transfer tofu pieces to a cutting board, then let them cool and cut into small pieces, set aside until required.
6. Return skillet pan over medium heat, add garlic and ginger and cook for 1 to 2 minutes or until fragrant.
7. Return tofu pieces into the pan, season with five-spice mix, add ½ tablespoon coriander, stir well and transfer tofu to a bowl, set aside until required.
8. When the timer beeps, press 'cancel' button and do quick pressure release until pressure nob drops down.
9. Open the instant pot and stir barley and check it, barley must be tender.
10. Return skillet pan over medium heat, add remaining oil in it, then add onion, zucchini, and peppers and cook for 5 to 6 minutes or until softened.
11. Add peas and cooked barley mixture and stir well.
12. Divide barley evenly between serving plates, top with tofu, garnish with coriander, then drizzle with soy sauce and scatter pomegranate seeds on top.
13. Serve straight away.

Barley and Wild Mushroom Risotto

Servings: 4
Preparation time: 20 minutes
Cooking time: 25 minutes

Nutrition Value:

Calories: 305 Cal, Carbs: 56 g, Fat: 4.4 g, Protein: 8.5 g, Fiber: 3.7 g.

Ingredients:

- 8.8-ounce pearl barley, uncooked
- 14-ounce mixed mushrooms, sliced
- 1 medium white onion, peeled and chopped
- 1 medium red pepper, chopped
- 1 teaspoon minced garlic
- ¼ teaspoon ground white pepper
- ¼ teaspoon cracked black pepper
- 1 tablespoon chopped fresh basil
- 1 teaspoon dried oregano
- 2 teaspoons olive oil
- 3 cups vegetable stock
- 4 tablespoons soy-based cream

Method:

1. Plugin instant pot, insert the inner pot, press sauté/simmer button and when hot, add oil and onion and cook for 1 minute or until onion begins to soften.
2. Add garlic and red pepper, continue cooking for 2 minutes, then add mushrooms and cook for 3 minutes.
3. Reserve some of the mushroom, then add remaining mushrooms into the instant pot along with barley, oregano and white pepper, pour in the stock and stir well.
4. Press the cancel button, shut the instant pot with its lid and turn the pressure knob to seal the pot.
5. Press the 'manual' button, then press the 'timer' to set the cooking time to 16 minutes and cook at high pressure, instant pot will take 5 minutes or more for building its inner pressure.
6. When the timer beeps, press 'cancel' button and do natural pressure release for 10 minutes and then do quick pressure release until pressure nob drops down.
7. Open the instant pot, stir barley, then stir in cream until combined and top with basil.
8. Sprinkle black pepper over risotto, scatter with reserved mushrooms and serve.

Chicken, Pasta and Spinach Soup

Servings: 4
Preparation time: 20 minutes
Cooking time: 10 minutes

Nutrition Value:

Calories: 260 Cal, Carbs: 15 g, Fat: 10 g, Protein: 26 g, Fiber: 3 g.

Ingredients:

- 2-ounces rotini pasta, wholegrain
- 2 cups cooked chicken breast, diced
- 1 cup baby spinach
- 14.5-ounce diced tomatoes
- 1/4 teaspoon salt
- 1/4 cup fresh basil, chopped
- 1 tablespoon olive oil
- 2 tablespoons grated Parmesan cheese
- 14-ounce chicken broth

Method:

1. Plugin instant pot, insert the inner pot, add pasta, tomato, and broth and stir until mixed.
2. Shut the instant pot with its lid and turn the pressure knob to seal the pot.
3. Press the 'manual' button, then press the 'timer' to set the cooking time to 5 minutes and cook at high pressure, instant pot will take 5 minutes or more for building its inner pressure.
4. When the timer beeps, press 'cancel' button and do quick pressure release until pressure nob drops down.
5. Open the instant pot, add remaining ingredients except for cheese and stir until mixed.
6. Shut instant pot with lid, let pasta stand for 5 minutes or until it absorbs all the flavors.
7. Divide pasta evenly between bowls, top with cheese and serve.

Black and Pinto Bean Chili

Servings: 8
Preparation time: 15 minutes
Cooking time: 4 hours

Nutrition Value:

Calories: 217 Cal, Carbs: 26.8 g, Fat: 4.7 g, Protein: 18.9 g, Fiber: 8.3 g.

Ingredients:

- 1-pound ground turkey
- 14.5-ounce cooked black beans
- 14.5-ounce cooked pinto beans
- 1 green pepper, seeded & chopped
- 28-ounce diced tomatoes
- 1 medium white onion, peeled and chopped
- 1 teaspoon minced garlic
- 1½ teaspoon ground black pepper
- teaspoon chopped oregano
- 1 1/2 teaspoons cayenne pepper
- ½ teaspoon cumin
- 1 cup vegetable stock

Method:

1. Plugin instant pot, insert the inner pot, press sauté/simmer button and when hot, add turkey along with remaining ingredients and stir until mixed.
2. Shut the instant pot with its lid and turn the pressure knob to seal the pot.
3. Press the 'slow cook' button, then press the 'timer' to set the cooking time to 4 hours at low heat setting.
4. When the timer beeps, press 'cancel' button and do natural pressure release for 10 minutes and then do quick pressure release until pressure nob drops down.
5. Open the instant pot, stir the chili and then evenly divide into serving bowls.
6. Serve straight away.

Black Beans, Corn, and Cheese on Sweet Potato

Servings: 6
Preparation time: 20 minutes
Cooking time: 15 minutes

Nutrition Value:

Calories: 194 Cal, Carbs: 61.5 g, Fat: 3.1 g, Protein: 9.6 g, Fiber: 11.3 g.

Ingredients:

- 6 medium sweet potato
- 14-ounce cooked black beans
- 15.25-ounce cooked corn
- 1/3 cup shredded sharp cheddar
- 1 cup water

Method:

1. Plugin instant pot, insert the inner pot, pour in water, then insert steamer basket and place sweet potatoes on it.
2. Shut the instant pot with its lid and turn the pressure knob to seal the pot.
3. Press the 'steam' button, then press the 'timer' to set the cooking time to 10 minutes and cook at high pressure, instant pot will take 5 minutes or more for building its inner pressure.
4. When the timer beeps, press 'cancel' button and do natural pressure release or until pressure nob drops down.
5. Then open the instant pot, remove sweet potatoes, and let cool enough to be handled by hands.
6. Peel the sweet potatoes, cut into bite-size pieces, then place in a bowl and mash with form until smooth.
7. Divide mashed sweet potatoes evenly between six plates, evenly top with beans and corn and sprinkle with cheese.
8. Serve straight away.

Chicken Pea Curry

Servings: 2
Preparation time: 10 minutes
Cooking time: 27 minutes

Nutrition Value:

Calories: 212 Cal, Carbs: 39 g, Fat: 3.6 g, Protein: 9.8 g, Fiber: 4.3 g.

Ingredients:

- 1 cup chickpeas, uncooked
- 1 medium white onion, peeled and chopped
- 2 medium green chilies, chopped
- 1 medium tomato, chopped
- 2 teaspoons minced garlic
- 1 teaspoon grated ginger
- 1 teaspoon salt
- 1 teaspoon red chili powder
- 1 teaspoon coriander powder
- 1 teaspoon garam masala
- 1 teaspoon turmeric powder
- 3 bay leaves
- 3 tablespoons olive oil
- 1 tablespoon chopped parsley
- 2 cups water

Method:

1. Plugin instant pot, insert the inner pot, and add chickpeas and 1 ¼ cup water.
2. Shut the instant pot with its lid and turn the pressure knob to seal the pot.
3. Press the 'manual' button, then press the 'timer' to set the cooking time to 12 minutes and cook at high pressure, instant pot will take 5 minutes or more for building its inner pressure.
4. When the timer beeps, press 'cancel' button and do natural pressure release for 5 minutes and then do quick pressure release until pressure nob drops down.
5. Then open the instant pot, drain chickpeas, and set aside.
6. Place a skillet pan over medium heat, add oil and bay leaves and fry for 30 seconds.

7. Stir in ginger and garlic paste and cook for 1 minute or until nicely golden brown and fragrant.
8. Season with salt, chili powder, coriander, garam masala, and turmeric, continue cooking for 3 minutes, then pour in remaining water and bring the gravy to boil.
9. Then add cooked chickpeas, stir well, and cook for 5 minutes, covering the pan.
10. Serve straight away.

Yellow Lentils

Servings: 4
Preparation time: 10 minutes
Cooking time: 20 minutes

Nutrition Value:

Calories: 55.6 Cal, Carbs: 6.2 g, Fat: 2.6 g, Protein: 2.5 g, Fiber: 2.2 g.

Ingredients:

- ½ cup yellow lentils
- 1 green chili, chopped
- ½ teaspoon salt
- ½ teaspoon mustard seeds
- ½ teaspoon cumin seeds
- ½ of a lemon, juiced
- 1 tablespoon olive oil
- 2 cups water
- 1 tablespoon chopped cilantro

Method:

1. Plugin instant pot, insert the inner pot, add lentils and pour in 1 cup water.
2. Shut the instant pot with its lid and turn the pressure knob to seal the pot.
3. Press the 'manual' button, then press the 'timer' to set the cooking time to 5 minutes and cook at high pressure, instant pot will take 5 minutes or more for building its inner pressure.
4. When the timer beeps, press 'cancel' button and do natural pressure release for 5 minutes and then do quick pressure release until pressure nob drops down.
5. Open the instant pot, add salt, green chilies and remaining water and stir until mixed.
6. Press the 'sauté/simmer' button and cook lentils for 5 minutes or more until boil.
7. Meanwhile, place a skillet pan over medium heat, add oil and when hot, add cumin seeds and mustard seeds and cook for 1 to 2 minutes or until fragrant.
8. Carefully, add seed mixture into lentils and press the cancel button.
9. Add lemon juice, stir well and then garnish with cilantro.
10. Serve straight away.

Seasoned Beans, Rice, and Vegetables

Servings: 6
Preparation time: 5 minutes
Cooking time: 35 minutes

Nutrition Value:

Calories: 198 Cal, Carbs: 7 g, Fat: 3 g, Protein: 10 g, Fiber: 7 g.

Ingredients:

- 3 cups mixed vegetables, frozen
- 1 cup split mung bean, uncooked
- 1 cup brown rice
- 1 teaspoon salt
- 1 tablespoon curry powder
- 1 tablespoon olive oil
- 4 cups water

Method:

1. Plugin instant pot, insert the inner pot, add all the ingredients, and stir until mixed.
2. Shut the instant pot with its lid and turn the pressure knob to seal the pot.
3. Press the 'manual' button, then press the 'timer' to set the cooking time to 30 minutes and cook at high pressure, instant pot will take 5 minutes or more for building its inner pressure.
4. When the timer beeps, press 'cancel' button and do quick pressure release until pressure nob drops down.
5. Open the instant pot, stir the bean-rice mixture and check if it cooked, if not then cook for another 10 minutes.
6. Serve straight away.

Wheat Berry, Black Bean, and Avocado Salad

Servings: 4
Preparation time: 10 minutes
Cooking time: 30 minutes

Nutrition Value:

Calories: 320 Cal, Carbs: 33 g, Fat: 17 g, Protein: 13 g, Fiber: 9 g.

Ingredients:

- 1/3 cup dried black beans
- 1/2 cup wheat berries, uncooked
- 1 medium avocado, peeled, pitted and chopped
- 2 cups grape tomatoes
- 1 cup chopped poblano pepper
- ½ cup chopped fresh cilantro
- 1 teaspoon minced garlic
- ½ teaspoon salt
- 4 cups water
- 2 tablespoons apple cider vinegar
- 2 tablespoons olive oil
- 3-ounce shredded cheddar cheese

Method:

1. Plugin instant pot, insert the inner pot, add black beans and wheat berries and then pour in water.
2. Press the cancel button, shut the instant pot with its lid and turn the pressure knob to seal the pot.
3. Press the 'manual' button, then press the 'timer' to set the cooking time to 25 minutes and cook at high pressure, instant pot will take 5 minutes or more for building its inner pressure.
4. Meanwhile, place tomato and pepper in a bowl, add garlic and cilantro, season with salt, then drizzle with vinegar and oil and stir until mixed.
5. When the timer beeps, press 'cancel' button, do quick pressure release until pressure nob drops down.
6. Open the instant pot, drain the wheat and berries, rinse under cold water, then drain well and place in a large bowl.
7. Add tomato and pepper mixture, then add avocado and cheese and toss until evenly mixed.
8. Serve straight away.

Cauliflower Fried Rice

Servings: 6
Preparation time: 10 minutes
Cooking time: 15 minutes

Nutrition Value:

Calories: 418 Cal, Carbs: 18 g, Fat: 26 g, Protein: 28 g, Fiber: 5 g.

Ingredients:

- 1 large head of cauliflower, cut into florets and riced
- 1 cup frozen peas and carrots mix, thawed
- 1/2 teaspoon garlic powder
- 1/4 teaspoon ground black pepper
- 1 tablespoon soy sauce
- 2 tablespoons sesame oil
- 2 eggs, beaten
- 2 tablespoons chopped scallions

Method:

1. Plugin instant pot, insert the inner pot, press sauté/simmer button and when hot, add oil and when hot, add cauliflower rice, peas, and carrots and cook for 5 minutes.
2. Press the cancel button, add garlic powder, black pepper and soy sauce, stir until combined, then shut the instant pot with its lid and turn the pressure knob to seal the pot.
3. Press the 'manual' button, then press the 'timer' to set the cooking time to 1 minute and cook at high pressure, instant pot will take 5 minutes or more for building its inner pressure.
4. When the timer beeps, press 'cancel' button and do quick pressure release until pressure nob drops down.
5. Open the instant pot, stir cauliflower rice mixture and then push to one side of the pot.
6. Press the sauté button, spray empty side of the pot with oil and slowly pour beaten eggs in that place.
7. Cook eggs for 3 minutes or until scrambled and then stir with cauliflower rice until well mixed.
8. Serve straight away.

Baked Butternut Squash

Servings: 12
Preparation time: 5 minutes
Cooking time: 15 minutes

Nutrition Value:

Calories: 113 Cal, Carbs: 16 g, Fat: 5 g, Protein: 2 g, Fiber: 5 g.

Ingredients:

- 5 pounds butternut squash
- 1/4 teaspoon ground cinnamon
- 1/8 teaspoon salt
- 1/8 teaspoon ground black pepper
- 2 tablespoons olive oil

Method:

1. Peel butternut squash, then remove its seed and cut into 3/4-inch pieces.
2. Plugin instant pot, insert the inner pot, press sauté/simmer button and when hot, add oil and when hot, add butternut squash pieces in a single layer.
3. Cook butternut squash pieces for 5 minutes or until nicely golden brown, then transfer to a plate and cook remaining butternut squash in the same manner.
4. Return browned butternut squash pieces into the instant pot, press the cancel button, shut the instant pot with its lid and turn the pressure knob to seal the pot.
5. Press the 'manual' button, then press the 'timer' to set the cooking time to 5 minutes and cook at high pressure, instant pot will take 5 minutes or more for building its inner pressure.
6. When the timer beeps, press 'cancel' button and do quick pressure release until pressure nob drops down.
7. Open the instant pot, transfer butternut squash toa serving plate, season with salt and black pepper and serve immediately.

Mac and Cheese

Servings: 2
Preparation time: 10 minutes
Cooking time: 15 minutes

Nutrition Value:

Calories: 478 Cal, Carbs: 69 g, Fat: 9.3 g, Protein: 24 g, Fiber: 10.7 g.

Ingredients:

- ½ cup macaroni, uncooked
- 2 medium white onions, peeled and chopped
- 1 leek, sliced into rings
- ½ cup frozen peas
- ½ teaspoon garlic powder
- 1 teaspoon Dijon mustard
- 1 teaspoon olive oil
- ¾ cup milk
- 1 cup vegetable stock
- 2 tablespoons grated cheddar cheese

Method:

1. Plugin instant pot, insert the inner pot, press sauté/simmer button and when hot, add oil and when hot, add leek and onion and cook for 5 to 7 minutes or until softened.
2. Then add garlic powder, mustard, pasta, vegetable stock, and stir until mixed.
3. Press the cancel button, shut the instant pot with its lid and turn the pressure knob to seal the pot.
4. Press the 'manual' button, then press the 'timer' to set the cooking time to 4 minutes and cook at high pressure, instant pot will take 5 minutes or more for building its inner pressure.
5. When the timer beeps, press 'cancel' button and do quick pressure release until pressure nob drops down.
6. Open the instant pot, add remaining ingredients, stir until mixed and let rest for 5 minutes or until peas are softened.
7. Serve straight away.

Roast Vegetable and Bean Stew

Servings: 6
Preparation time: 10 minutes
Cooking time: 10 minutes

Nutrition Value:

Calories: 278 Cal, Carbs: 58 g, Fat: 3 g, Protein: 8 g, Fiber: 11 g.

Ingredients:

- 19-ounce cooked pinto beans
- 1 small butternut squash
- 1-pound potatoes
- 2 large zucchinis
- 2 medium carrots
- 2 medium parsnips
- 1 teaspoon minced garlic
- 1 ½ teaspoon salt
- ¾ teaspoon ground black pepper
- 4 large sprigs of rosemary
- 1 cup apple cider
- 2 teaspoons olive oil
- 1 cup vegetable broth

Method:

1. Peel squash, potatoes, zucchini, carrot, and parsnips, then cut into 1 ½ inch pieces and place into the inner pot of instant pot.
2. Plugin instant pot, add remaining ingredients except for beans and stir until mixed, then shut the instant pot with its lid and turn the pressure knob to seal the pot.
3. Press the 'manual' button, then press the 'timer' to set the cooking time to 3 minutes and cook at high pressure, instant pot will take 5 minutes or more for building its inner pressure.
4. When the timer beeps, press 'cancel' button and do quick pressure release until pressure nob drops down.
5. Open the instant pot, add kidney beans, stir until well mixed, then shut instant pot with a lid and let rest for 10 minutes.
6. Serve straight away.

Pea and Cottage Cheese Curry

Servings: 4
Preparation time: 10 minutes
Cooking time: 18 minutes

Nutrition Value:

Calories: 294 Cal, Carbs: 12 g, Fat: 18 g, Protein: 21 g, Fiber: 4 g.

Ingredients:

- 1 ½ cups chopped white onions
- 1 cup chopped tomatoes
- 12-ounce frozen peas
- 1 tablespoon minced garlic
- 1 tablespoon grated ginger
- 1 teaspoon cayenne pepper
- 1 teaspoon turmeric powder
- 1 teaspoon garam masala
- 2 tablespoons olive oil
- ¼ cup coconut milk, reduced-fat and unsweetened
- ¾ cup water
- 1 cup chopped cottage cheese
- 1/4 cup chopped cilantro

Method:

1. Plugin instant pot, insert the inner pot, add onion and tomatoes along with garlic and ginger, then sprinkle with cayenne pepper, turmeric, and garam masala, drizzle with oil and pour in ¼ cup water.
2. Stir the ingredients, then shut the instant pot with its lid and turn the pressure knob to seal the pot.
3. Press the 'manual' button, then press the 'timer' to set the cooking time to 5 minutes and cook at high pressure, instant pot will take 5 minutes or more for building its inner pressure.
4. When the timer beeps, press 'cancel' button and do natural pressure release for 5 minutes and then do quick pressure release until pressure nob drops down.
5. Open the instant pot, select the 'sauté' button, add all the remaining ingredients, stir well and cook for 5 to 8 minutes or until heated through.
6. Serve straight away.

Chapter8: Sides

Pinto Beans

Servings: 10
Preparation time: 20 minutes
Cooking time: 55 minutes

Nutrition Value:

Calories: 62.1 Cal, Carbs: 11.7 g, Fat: 0.2 g, Protein: 3.7 g, Fiber: 4 g.

Ingredients:

- 2 cups pinto beans, dried
- 1 medium white onion, peeled and diced
- 1 ½ teaspoon minced garlic
- ¾ teaspoon salt
- 1/4 teaspoon ground black pepper
- 1 teaspoon red chili powder
- 1/4 teaspoon cumin
- 1 tablespoon olive oil
- 1 teaspoon chopped cilantro
- 5 ½ cup vegetable stock

Method:

1. Plugin instant pot, insert the inner pot, press sauté/simmer button, add oil and when hot, add onion and garlic and cook for 3 minutes or until onions begin to soften.
2. Add remaining ingredients, stir well, then press the cancel button, shut the instant pot with its lid and turn the pressure knob to seal the pot.
3. Press the 'manual' button, then press the 'timer' to set the cooking time to 45 minutes and cook at high pressure, instant pot will take 5 minutes or more for building its inner pressure.
4. When the timer beeps, press 'cancel' button and do natural pressure release for 10 minutes until pressure nob drops down.
5. Open the instant pot, spoon beans into plates and serve.

Tuna Melt

Servings: 2
Preparation time: 10 minutes
Cooking time: 10 minutes

Nutrition Value:

Calories: 306.1 Cal, Carbs: 27.5 g, Fat: 5.5 g, Protein: 35 g, Fiber: 3.8 g.

Ingredients:

- 8-ounce tuna fillet
- 2 whole-wheat English muffins, halved
- 1 green onion, sliced
- ½ teaspoon ground black pepper
- 1 tablespoon dried dill weed
- 1 tablespoon Dijon mustard
- 3/4 cup Coleslaw mix
- 1 ½ tablespoons mayonnaise
- 1/3 cup grated cheddar cheese
- 1 cup water

Method:

1. Plugin instant pot, insert the inner pot, pour in water, then insert steamer basket and place tuna on it.
2. Shut the instant pot with its lid, turn the pressure knob to seal the pot, press the 'steam' button, then press the 'timer' to set the cooking time to 4 minutes and cook at high pressure, instant pot will take 5 minutes or more for building its inner pressure.
3. Meanwhile, place remaining ingredients except for cheese and muffins in a large bowl and stir until mixed.
4. When the timer beeps, press 'cancel' button and do natural pressure release for 5 minutes and then do quick pressure release until pressure nob drops down.
5. Open the instant pot, then transfer tuna to a cutting board, let cool for 10 minutes and then shred with two forks.
6. Add shredded tuna to mayonnaise mixture and stir until combined.
7. Cut muffins into half, then top evenly with tuna mixture and sprinkle with cheese.
8. Place muffins under the broiler and cook for 4 to 5 minutes or until cheese melts.
9. Serve straight away.

Collard Greens

Servings: 12
Preparation time: 5 minutes
Cooking time: 6 hours and 5 minutes

Nutrition Value:

Calories: 49.6 Cal, Carbs: 2.3 g, Fat: 3.1 g, Protein: 3.4 g, Fiber: 0.5 g.

Ingredients:

- 2 pounds chopped collard greens
- ¾ cup chopped white onion
- 1 teaspoon onion powder
- 1 teaspoon garlic powder
- 1 teaspoon salt
- 2 teaspoons brown sugar
- ½ teaspoon ground black pepper
- ½ teaspoon red chili powder
- ¼ teaspoon crushed red pepper flakes
- 3 tablespoons apple cider vinegar
- 2 tablespoons olive oil
- 14.5-ounce vegetable broth
- 1/2 cup water

Method:

1. Plugin instant pot, insert the inner pot, add onion and collard and then pour in vegetable broth and water.
2. Shut the instant pot with its lid, turn the pressure knob to seal the pot, press the 'slow cook' button, then press the 'timer' to set the cooking time to 6 hours at high heat setting.
3. When the timer beeps, press 'cancel' button and do natural pressure release until pressure nob drops down.
4. Open the instant pot, add remaining ingredients and stir until mixed.
5. Then press the 'sauté/simmer' button and cook for 3 to 5 minutes or more until collards reach to desired texture.
6. Serve straight away.

Chili Lime Salmon

Servings: 2
Preparation time: 5 minutes
Cooking time: 10 minutes

Nutrition Value:

Calories: 305 Cal, Carbs: 29 g, Fat: 5 g, Protein: 36 g, Fiber: 8 g.

Ingredients:

For Sauce:

- 1 jalapeno pepper, deseeded and diced
- 1 tablespoon chopped parsley
- 1 teaspoon minced garlic
- 1/2 teaspoon cumin
- 1/2 teaspoon paprika
- 1/2 teaspoon lime zest
- 1 tablespoon honey
- 1 tablespoon lime juice
- 1 tablespoon olive oil
- 1 tablespoon water

For Fish:

- 2 salmon fillets, each about 5 ounces
- 1 cup water
- 1/2 teaspoon salt
- 1/8 teaspoon ground black pepper

Method:

1. Prepare salmon and for this, season salmon with salt and black pepper until evenly coated.
2. Plugin instant pot, insert the inner pot, pour in water, then place steamer basket and place seasoned salmon on it.
3. Shut the instant pot with its lid, turn the pressure knob to seal the pot, press the 'steam' button, then press the 'timer' to set the cooking time to 5 minutes and cook

at high pressure, instant pot will take 5 minutes or more for building its inner pressure.

4. Meanwhile, place all the ingredients for the sauce in a bowl, whisk until combined and set aside until required.

5. When the timer beeps, press 'cancel' button and do quick pressure release until pressure nob drops down.

6. Open the instant pot, then transfer salmon to a serving plate and drizzle generously with prepared sauce.

7. Serve straight away.

Quinoa Tabbouleh

Servings: 6
Preparation time: 5 minutes
Cooking time: 16 minutes

Nutrition Value:

Calories: 283.6 Cal, Carbs: 30.6 g, Fat: 16.1 g, Protein: 5.8 g, Fiber: 3.4 g.

Ingredients:

- 1 cup quinoa, rinsed
- 1 large English cucumber, cut into ¼-inch pieces
- 2 scallions, sliced
- 2 cups cherry tomatoes, halved
- 2/3 cup chopped parsley
- 1/2 cup chopped mint
- ½ teaspoon minced garlic
- 1/2 teaspoon salt
- ½ teaspoon ground black pepper
- 2 tablespoon lemon juice
- 1/2 cup olive oil

Method:

1. Plugin instant pot, insert the inner pot, add quinoa, then pour in water and stir until mixed.
2. Shut the instant pot with its lid and turn the pressure knob to seal the pot.
3. Press the 'manual' button, then press the 'timer' to set the cooking time to 1 minute and cook at high pressure, instant pot will take 5 minutes or more for building its inner pressure.
4. When the timer beeps, press 'cancel' button and do natural pressure release for 10 minutes and then do quick pressure release until pressure nob drops down.
5. Open the instant pot, fluff quinoa with a fork, then spoon it on a rimmed baking sheet, spread quinoa evenly and let cool.
6. Meanwhile, place lime juice in a small bowl, add garlic and stir until just mixed.
7. Then add salt, black pepper, and olive oil and whisk until combined.
8. Transfer cooled quinoa to a large bowl, add remaining ingredients, then drizzle generously with the prepared lime juice mixture and toss until evenly coated.
9. Taste quinoa to adjust seasoning and then serve.

Lemon Hummus

Servings: 6
Preparation time: 15 minutes
Cooking time: 40 minutes

Nutrition Value:

Calories: 70 Cal, Carbs: 4 g, Fat: 5 g, Protein: 2 g, Fiber: 1 g.

Ingredients:

- 1-pound chickpeas, dried
- 2 lemons, juiced
- 1 tablespoon chopped parsley
- 1 teaspoon minced garlic
- 1/8 teaspoon salt
- 2 tablespoons olive oil
- 1/4 cup tahini paste
- 1/2 of lemon, zested
- 12 cups water

Method:

1. Plugin instant pot, insert the inner pot, add chickpeas, and pour in water.
2. Shut the instant pot with its lid, turn the pressure knob to seal the pot, press the 'manual' button, then press the 'timer' to set the cooking time to 35 minutes and cook at high pressure, instant pot will take 5 minutes or more for building its inner pressure.
3. When the timer beeps, press 'cancel' button and do natural pressure release for 10 minutes and then do quick pressure release until pressure nob drops down.
4. Open the instant pot, drain chick peas, and transfer to a food processor.
5. Add remaining ingredients except for lemon zest and parsley and pulse chickpeas for 1 to 2 minutes or until smooth, frequently scraping the sides of a food processor.
6. Add water if the hummus is too thick, then tip it in a bowl and garnish with lemon zest and parsley.
7. Serve straight away.

Tomato Ketchup

Servings: 6
Preparation time: 20 minutes
Cooking time: 20 minutes

Nutrition Value:

Calories: 14 Cal, Carbs: 3.6 g, Fat: 0.1 g, Protein: 0.2 g, Fiber: 0.8 g.

Ingredients:

- 50-ounce tomatoes, quartered
- 2 mushrooms, diced
- 1/4 teaspoon onion powder
- 2 teaspoons powdered erythritol
- 1/4 teaspoon garlic powder
- 1/4 teaspoon allspice
- 4 tablespoons white vinegar

Method:

1. Plugin instant pot, insert the inner pot, add all the ingredients, and stir until mixed.
2. Shut the instant pot with its lid, turn the pressure knob to seal the pot, press the 'manual' button, then press the 'timer' to set the cooking time to 10 minutes and cook at high pressure, instant pot will take 5 minutes or more for building its inner pressure.
3. When the timer beeps, press 'cancel' button and do natural pressure release for 10 minutes and then do quick pressure release until pressure nob drops down.
4. Open the instant pot, puree the mixture until smooth and then press 'sauté/simmer' button to cook ketchup for 5 minutes or until thickened to desired consistency.
5. When done, ladle ketchup into a jar, let cool completely and serve.

Chickpea Salad

Servings: 6
Preparation time: 5 minutes
Cooking time: 40 minutes

Nutrition Value:

Calories: 301 Cal, Carbs: 37 g, Fat: 13 g, Protein: 11 g, Fiber: 10 g.

Ingredients:

- 1 cup chickpeas, dried
- 3 cups water
- 1/4 cup chopped green bell pepper
- 10 black olives, pitted and halved
- 10 cherry tomatoes, halved
- 2 tablespoons chopped cilantro
- 1 medium cucumber, 1/2-inch dice
- 1/2 cup chopped white onion
- 2 tablespoons crumbled feta cheese
  For Dressing:
- 1 teaspoon salt
- 1/2 teaspoon ground black pepper
- 1 tablespoon red wine vinegar
- 2 tablespoons olive oil

Method:
1. Plugin instant pot, insert the inner pot, add chickpeas, and pour in water.
2. Shut the instant pot with its lid, turn the pressure knob to seal the pot, press the 'manual' button, then press the 'timer' to set the cooking time to 35 minutes and cook at high pressure, instant pot will take 5 minutes or more for building its inner pressure.
3. Meanwhile, whisk together all the ingredients for the dressing and set aside until required.
4. When the timer beeps, press 'cancel' button and do quick pressure release until pressure nob drops down.
5. Open the instant pot, drain the chickpeas, let cool for 20 minutes and then transfer into a salad bowl.
6. Drizzle chickpeas with prepared salad dressing, then add remaining ingredients and toss until well coated.
7. Chill salad in the refrigerator for 30 minutes and then serve.

Chapter9: Poultry

Turkey Chili

Servings: 6
Preparation time: 20 minutes
Cooking time: 40 minutes

Nutrition Value:

Calories: 220 Cal, Carbs: 22 g, Fat: 7 g, Protein: 20 g, Fiber: 5 g.

Ingredients:

- 1 1/2 cup frozen corn
- 15-ounce cooked black beans
- 1-pound ground turkey
- 14.5-ounce diced tomatoes
- 1 teaspoon garlic powder
- ¾ teaspoon salt
- 2 tablespoons red chili powder
- 1 tablespoon cumin
- 1 ½ teaspoon smoked paprika
- 1 teaspoon dried basil
- 1 teaspoon oregano
- 1 cup water

Method:

1. Plugin instant pot, insert the inner pot, add turkey, and then add remaining ingredients.
2. Shut the instant pot with its lid, turn the pressure knob to seal the pot, then press the 'manual' button, then press the 'timer' to set the cooking time to 25 minutes and cook at high pressure, instant pot will take 5 minutes or more for building its inner pressure.
3. When the timer beeps, press 'cancel' button and do quick pressure release until pressure nob drops down.
4. Open the instant pot, stir the chili and evenly divide between serving bowls.
5. Serve straight away.

Chicken Stuffed Potatoes

Servings: 4
Preparation time: 10 minutes
Cooking time: 30 minutes

Nutrition Value:

Calories: 350 Cal, Carbs: 45 g, Fat: 12 g, Protein: 16 g, Fiber: 6 g.

Ingredients:

- 6-ounce chicken sausage links
- 4 medium potatoes, each about 8-ounce
- 1 medium zucchini, chopped
- 1 cup chopped green onion
- 1/8 teaspoon salt
- ¼ teaspoon ground black pepper
- ½ teaspoon dried oregano
- 1 teaspoon hot sauce
- 2 tablespoons olive oil, divided
- 2 cups water
- 2 tablespoons crumbled blue cheese, reduced fat

Method:

1. Plugin instant pot, insert the inner pot, press sauté/simmer button, add 1 tablespoon oil and when hot, add chicken sausage and cook for 3 minutes or until edges are nicely golden brown.
2. Add zucchini and ¾ cup green onion, sprinkle with oregano, pour in 1/3 cup water and cook for 3 minutes or until tender-crisp.
3. Then transfer vegetables from the instant pot to a bowl, drizzle with remaining oil and hot sauce, toss until mixed and keep warm by covering the bowl.
4. Press the cancel button, pour in the remaining water, then insert steamer basket and place potatoes on it.
5. Shut the instant pot with its lid, turn the pressure knob to seal the pot, press the 'manual' button, then press the 'timer' to set the cooking time to 18 minutes and cook at high pressure, instant pot will take 5 minutes or more for building its inner pressure.
6. When the timer beeps, press 'cancel' button and do quick pressure release until pressure nob drops down.

7. Open the instant pot, transfer potatoes to a plate, let cool for 5 minutes, then cut each potato in half.
8. Use fork to fluff potatoes, then season with salt and black pepper and evenly top with prepared sausage and zucchini mixture.
9. Sprinkle remaining green onions and cheese on loaded potatoes and serve straight away.

Lentils with Lamb

Servings: 10
Preparation time: 10 minutes
Cooking time: 25 minutes
Nutrition Value:
Calories: 126.3 Cal, Carbs: 20.7 g, Fat: 1.5 g, Protein: 14.6 g, Fiber: 8.9 g.
Ingredients:

- 1-pound lamb, cubed
- 1-pound lentils, dried
- 1-pound red lentils, dried
- 10-ounce frozen spinach
- 14-ounce crushed tomato
- 2 medium white onions, peeled and sliced
- 2 teaspoons minced garlic
- 1 teaspoon grated ginger
- 1 teaspoon salt
- 1 tablespoon ground black pepper
- 1 tablespoon curry powder
- 1 tablespoon ground coriander
- 1 tablespoon ground cumin
- 1 lime, juiced
- 1 cup beef stock
- Water as needed
- 1 cup low-fat yogurt

Method:

1. Stir together salt, black pepper, curry powder, coriander, and cumin and then sprinkle this spice mix generously on all sides of lamb pieces.
2. Plugin instant pot, insert the inner pot, add seasoned lamb pieces along with remaining ingredients except for yogurt, pour in water to cover all the ingredients and stir until just mixed.
3. Shut the instant pot with its lid, turn the pressure knob to seal the pot, press the 'manual' button, then press the 'timer' to set the cooking time to 20 minutes and cook at high pressure, instant pot will take 5 minutes or more for building its inner pressure.
4. When the timer beeps, press 'cancel' button and do quick pressure release until pressure nob drops down.
5. Open the instant pot, stir lamb and then stir in yogurt.
6. Serve straight away.

Chicken Tacos

Servings: 10
Preparation time: 35 minutes
Cooking time: 25 minutes

Nutrition Value:

Calories: 164.4 Cal, Carbs: 8.3 g, Fat: 11.1 g, Protein: 10.1 g, Fiber: 4.8 g.

Ingredients:

- 4 pounds chicken breast
- 1/2 of a medium head of lettuce, shredded
- 3 medium avocados, pitted and flesh chopped
- 1 medium white onion, peeled and chopped
- 3 limes, juiced
- 2 jalapeno peppers, deseeded and diced
- 1 teaspoon onion powder
- 1 teaspoon garlic powder
- 1 ¾ teaspoon salt
- 1 teaspoon ground black pepper
- 1 ½ teaspoon red chili powder
- 1 ½ teaspoon ground cumin
- 2 tablespoons olive oil

Method:

1. Place lettuce, avocado, onion, and pepper in a large bowl, drizzle with lime juice and toss until coated, chill vegetables in the refrigerator for 30 minutes.
2. Meanwhile, plug-in instant pot, insert the inner pot, pour in water, then insert trivet stand and place chicken on it.
3. Shut the instant pot with its lid, turn the pressure knob to seal the pot, press the 'manual' button, then press the 'timer' to set the cooking time to 10 minutes and cook at high pressure, instant pot will take 5 minutes or more for building its inner pressure.
4. When the timer beeps, press 'cancel' button and do quick pressure release until pressure nob drops down.
5. Open the instant pot, transfer chicken breasts to a cutting board, cool for 5 minutes, then shred with two forks.

6. Place shredded chicken in a bowl and season with salt, black pepper, red chili, and cumin until evenly coated.
7. Drain the instant pot, wipe clean the inner pot, then press the 'sauté/simmer' button, grease with oil and when hot, add seasoned chicken in a single layer and cook for 3 to 5 minutes or until chicken is nicely golden brown and slightly crispy.
8. Serve chicken in tortillas, topped with prepared vegetables.

Garlic Herb Chicken

Servings: 4
Preparation time: 5 minutes
Cooking time: 15 minutes

Nutrition Value:

Calories: 579 Cal, Carbs: 8 g, Fat: 12 g, Protein: 104 g, Fiber: 1 g.

Ingredients:

- 1-pound chicken breasts
- ½ teaspoon onion powder
- 1 teaspoon garlic powder
- 1 teaspoon salt
- ½ teaspoon ground black pepper
- ½ teaspoon dried thyme
- ½ teaspoon paprika
- ½ teaspoon dried basil
- ¾ cup water

Method:

1. Stir together salt, black pepper, thyme, paprika, and basil and sprinkle this spice mix generously all over the chicken until evenly coated.
2. Plugin instant pot, insert the inner pot, pour in water, then insert steamer basket and place seasoned chicken on it.
3. Shut the instant pot with its lid, turn the pressure knob to seal the pot, press the 'manual' button, then press the 'timer' to set the cooking time to 10 minutes and cook at high pressure, instant pot will take 5 minutes or more for building its inner pressure.
4. When the timer beeps, press 'cancel' button and do quick pressure release until pressure nob drops down.
5. Serve straight away.

Chicken & Rice

Servings: 6
Preparation time: 5 minutes
Cooking time: 4 hours and 40 minutes

Nutrition Value:

Calories: 128.7 Cal, Carbs: 9.5 g, Fat: 1.2 g, Protein: 19.3 g, Fiber: 0.8 g.

Ingredients:

- 1-pound chicken breast
- 3/4 cup brown rice, uncooked
- 1/2-pound mushrooms
- 1/2 cup sliced white onion
- 1/4 teaspoon salt
- 1 tablespoon olive oil
- 1 teaspoon poultry seasoning
- 2 cups chicken broth

Method:

1. Plugin instant pot, insert the inner pot, press sauté/simmer button, add oil and when hot, add onion, mushroom, and chicken and cook for 15 minutes or more until nicely golden brown on all sides.
2. Add remaining ingredients, except for rice, then press the cancel button, shut the instant pot with its lid and turn the pressure knob to seal the pot.
3. Press the 'slow cook' button, then press the 'timer' to set the cooking time to 4 hours and cook at low heat setting.
4. Then transfer chicken to a cutting board, add rice into the instant pot, stir well and continue cooking for 15 minutes or until rice is tender.
5. Meanwhile, let chicken cool for 10 minutes and then shred with two forks.
6. When rice is cooked, return chicken into the instant pot, stir well and continue cooking for 10 minutes or until warm through.
7. Serve straight away.

Pesto Chicken and Green Beans

Servings: 4
Preparation time: 10 minutes
Cooking time: 22 minutes

Nutrition Value:

Calories: 415 Cal, Carbs: 14 g, Fat: 16 g, Protein: 49 g, Fiber: 6 g.

Ingredients:

- 2 pounds green beans
- 4 medium chicken breasts
- 1 tablespoon garlic salt
- 2 tablespoons lemon pepper seasoning
- 2 tablespoons olive oil
- 6-ounce basil pesto
- 1 ½ cups chicken broth
- 2 cups water

Method:

1. Place beans in a large bowl, season with lemon pepper, then drizzle with oil and toss until well coated.
2. Plugin instant pot, insert the inner pot, pour in water, then insert steamer basket and place seasoned green beans on it.
3. Shut the instant pot with its lid, turn the pressure knob to seal the pot, press the 'manual' button, then press the 'timer' to set the cooking time to 2 minutes and cook at low pressure, instant pot will take 5 minutes or more for building its inner pressure.
4. When the timer beeps, press 'cancel' button and do quick pressure release until pressure nob drops down.
5. Open the instant pot and divide beans evenly between four plates, set aside until required.
6. Remove steamer basket from the instant pot, rinse the inner pot and pour in chicken broth.
7. Season chicken with garlic salt, add into the instant pot and shut the instant pot with its lid.

8. Turn the pressure knob to seal the pot, press the 'poultry' button, then press the 'timer' to set the cooking time to 15 minutes and cook at low pressure, instant pot will take 5 minutes or more for building its inner pressure.

9. When the timer beeps, press 'cancel' button and do quick pressure release until pressure nob drops down.

10. Open the instant pot, transfer chicken to a cutting board, let cool for 5 minutes and then shred chicken with two forks.

11. Drizzle pesto over shredded chicken, toss until evenly coated and evenly divide into plates containing green beans.

12. Serve straight away.

Turkey Burger Patty

Servings: 6
Preparation time: 5 minutes
Cooking time: 20 minutes

Nutrition Value:

Calories: 212 Cal, Carbs: 0 g, Fat: 14 g, Protein: 22 g, Fiber: 0 g.

Ingredients:

- 2 pounds ground turkey
- 2 teaspoons salt
- 1 teaspoon ground black pepper
- 1 teaspoon red chili powder
- ¾ teaspoon cumin
- 1 cup water

Method:

1. Place ground turkey in a large bowl, season with salt, black pepper, red chili powder and cumin and then shape mixture into six patties.
2. Plugin instant pot, insert the inner pot, pour in water, and then insert a steamer basket.
3. Wrap each patty with aluminum foil, place them on the steamer basket, then shut the instant pot with its lid and turn the pressure knob to seal the pot.
4. Press the 'manual' button, then press the 'timer' to set the cooking time to 15 minutes and cook at high pressure, instant pot will take 5 minutes or more for building its inner pressure.
5. When the timer beeps, press 'cancel' button and do quick pressure release until pressure nob drops down.
6. Open the instant pot, remove and uncover patties and serve.

Spinach Stuffed Chicken Breast

Servings: 4
Preparation time: 15 minutes
Cooking time: 20 minutes

Nutrition Value:

Calories: 262 Cal, Carbs: 8.5 g, Fat: 4.1 g, Protein: 46.1 g, Fiber: 2.4 g.

Ingredients:

- 4 chicken breasts
- 4 artichoke heart, chopped
- 4 teaspoons chopped sundried tomato
- 2 teaspoons minced garlic
- ¼ teaspoon ground black pepper
- 1 teaspoon curry powder
- 1 teaspoon paprika
- 20 basil leaves, chopped
- 4-ounce low-fat mozzarella cheese, chopped
- 1 cup water

Method:

1. Place artichoke heart in a bowl, add tomato, garlic, basil, and mozzarella cheese and stir until mixed.
2. Cut each chicken breast halfway through and then season chicken with salt, black pepper, curry powder, and paprika.
3. Stuff chicken with artichoke mixture and close the filling with chicken using a toothpick.
4. Plugin instant pot, insert the inner pot, pour in water, then insert steamer basket and place stuffed chicken breasts on it.
5. Shut the instant pot with its lid, turn the pressure knob to seal the pot, press the 'manual' button, then press the 'timer' to set the cooking time to 15 minutes and cook at high pressure, instant pot will take 5 minutes or more for building its inner pressure.
6. When the timer beeps, press 'cancel' button and do natural pressure release for 10 minutes and then do quick pressure release until pressure nob drops down.
7. Open the instant pot, transfer stuffed chicken to plates and serve.

Smoky Whole Chicken

Servings: 6
Preparation time: 15 minutes
Cooking time: 26 minutes

Nutrition Value:

Calories: 215 Cal, Carbs: 5 g, Fat: 9 g, Protein: 25 g, Fiber: 1 g.

Ingredients:

- 3 ½ pound whole chicken, giblets removed and rinsed
- 1 small onion, cut into four wedges
- 3 teaspoons minced garlic
- 1 tablespoon salt
- 1/4 teaspoon cayenne pepper
- 1 teaspoon ground black pepper
- 1 1/2 teaspoons smoked paprika
- 1/2 teaspoon herbes de Provence
- 2 tablespoons olive oil
- 1 large lemon, halved
- 1 cup Chicken Broth

Method:

1. Stir together salt, black pepper, cayenne pepper, paprika, herb de Provence and oil and then rub this mixture on the inside and outside of the chicken.
2. Stuff season chicken with onion wedges and lemon halves and tie chicken legs with kitchen twine.
3. Plugin instant pot, insert the inner pot, pour in chicken broth, insert steamer basket and place chicken on it, breast side up.
4. Shut the instant pot with its lid, turn the pressure knob to seal the pot, press the 'manual' button, then press the 'timer' to set the cooking time to 21 minutes and cook at high pressure, instant pot will take 5 minutes or more for building its inner pressure.
5. When the timer beeps, press 'cancel' button and do natural pressure release for 10 minutes and then do quick pressure release until pressure nob drops down.
6. Open the instant pot, transfer chicken to a cutting board and then cut into pieces.
7. Serve straight away.

Chapter10: Meat

Beef Stroganoff

Servings: 6
Preparation time: 20 minutes
Cooking time: 60 minutes

Nutrition Value:

Calories: 382.6 Cal, Carbs: 13.1 g, Fat: 17.9 g, Protein: 38.2 g, Fiber: 0.9 g.

Ingredients:

- 2 pounds beef steak
- 1/2 cup flour
- 2 cups sliced mushrooms
- 1 medium white onion, peeled and chopped
- 1 ½ teaspoon minced garlic
- 1/2 teaspoon salt
- 1 tablespoon Worcestershire sauce
- 1/4 teaspoon ground black pepper
- 3 tablespoons olive oil
- 14-ounce beef broth
- 1 cup sour cream

Method:

1. Cut beef into 1-inch pieces and then coat with ¼ cup flour.
2. Plugin instant pot, insert the inner pot, press sauté/simmer button, add oil and when hot, add coated beef pieces in a single layer and cook for 7 to 10 minutes or until nicely browned.
3. Cook remaining beef pieces in the same manner and then transfer to a bowl.
4. Then add onion and garlic and cook for 3 minutes or until sauté.
5. Add mushrooms, season with salt and black pepper, drizzle with Worcestershire sauce, pour in the broth, then return beef pieces and stir until mixed.
6. Press the cancel button, shut the instant pot with its lid and turn the pressure knob to seal the pot.

7. Press the 'manual' button, then press the 'timer' to set the cooking time to 30 minutes and cook at high pressure, instant pot will take 5 minutes or more for building its inner pressure.
8. When the timer beeps, press 'cancel' button and do natural pressure release for 10 minutes and then do quick pressure release until pressure nob drops down.
9. Open the lid, stir beef stroganoff and if the sauce is too thin, press the 'sauté/simmer' button and cook the sauce for 5 minutes or more until sauce is slightly thick.
10. Then press the cancel button, add sour cream into the instant pot and stir until combined.
11. Serve straight away.

Pork Roast

Servings: 6
Preparation time: 15 minutes
Cooking time: 50 minutes

Nutrition Value:

Calories: 478 Cal, Carbs: 9.5 g, Fat: 18.1 g, Protein: 66.1 g, Fiber: 2.7 g.

Ingredients:

- 2 pounds pork roast, fat trimmed
- 1 teaspoon garlic powder
- 2 teaspoons salt
- 1/2 teaspoon ground black pepper
- 1 teaspoon dried thyme
- 1 teaspoon dried rosemary
- 1 tablespoon oil
- 2 cups chicken broth

Method:

1. Stir together garlic, salt, black pepper, thyme, and rosemary and sprinkle this mixture on all sides of pork or until evenly coated.
2. Plugin instant pot, insert the inner pot, press the 'sauté/simmer' button, add 1 tablespoon oil and when hot, add seasoned pork and cook for 4 minutes per side.
3. When done, transfer pork to a plate, then pour in chicken broth and stir well to remove browned bits from the bottom of the instant pot.
4. Press the cancel button, insert trivet stand, place pork on it, then shut the instant pot with its lid and turn the pressure knob to seal the pot.
5. Press the 'meat/stew' button, then press the 'timer' to set the cooking time to 30 minutes and cook at high pressure, instant pot will take 5 minutes or more for building its inner pressure.
6. When the timer beeps, press 'cancel' button and do natural pressure release for 10 minutes and then do quick pressure release until pressure nob drops down.
7. Open the instant pot, transfer pork to a cutting board and let rest for 10 minutes.
8. Cut pork into even slices and serve.

Beef and Rice Stuffed Bell Peppers

Servings: 6
Preparation time: 15 minutes
Cooking time: 30 minutes
Nutrition Value:
Calories: 306 Cal, Carbs: 9 g, Fat: 14 g, Protein: 33 g, Fiber: 3.4 g.
Ingredients:

- 1 ½ cups rice, uncooked
- 4 large green peppers, deseeded and halved
- 1-pound ground beef
- 1 medium white onion, peeled and diced
- 1 medium tomato, diced
- ½ teaspoon salt
- ¼ teaspoon ground black pepper
- 2 cups beef broth
- ¼ cup water
- 1 tablespoon coconut oil

Method:

1. Plugin instant pot, insert the inner pot, press sauté/simmer button, add oil and when hot, add onion and cook for 5 minutes or until nicely golden brown.
2. Then add beef along with tomatoes, season with salt and black pepper, stir well and cook beef for 5 to 7 minutes or until nicely browned.
3. Add rice, pour in water, stir well and press the cancel button.
4. Shut the instant pot with its lid, turn the pressure knob to seal the pot, press the 'manual' button, then press the 'timer' to set the cooking time to 8 minutes and cook at high pressure, instant pot will take 5 minutes or more for building its inner pressure.
5. When the timer beeps, press 'cancel' button and do quick pressure release until pressure nob drops down.
6. Open the instant pot, stir well and stuff the rice-beef mixture into a bell pepper.
7. Remove a ¼ cup of the cooking liquid from the instant pot, then arrange stuffed pepper into the pan and shut with lid.
8. Press the 'manual' button, then press the 'timer' to set the cooking time to 4 minutes and cook at high pressure, instant pot will take 5 minutes or more for building its inner pressure.
9. When the timer beeps, press 'cancel' button and do quick pressure release until pressure nob drops down.
10. Serve straight away.

Beef Goulash

Servings: 8
Preparation time: 15 minutes
Cooking time: 45 minutes

Nutrition Value:

Calories: 315 Cal, Carbs: 17 g, Fat: 17 g, Protein: 24 g, Fiber: 2 g.

Ingredients:

- 2 pounds beef roast, cut into 1-inch cubes
- 6 medium carrots, peeled and cut into 1-inch pieces
- 1 medium white onion, peeled and cut into 1-inch pieces
- 2 teaspoon salt
- 1/4 cup cornstarch
- 2 tablespoons onion soup mix
- 2 teaspoons paprika
- 2 teaspoons Worcestershire sauce
- 2 cups beef broth
- 2 tablespoon olive oil
- 1/3 cup water

Method:

1. Cut beef into 1-inch cubes and season with salt.
2. Plugin instant pot, insert the inner pot, press sauté/simmer button, add oil and when hot, add seasoned beef pieces in a single layer and cook for 4 minutes per side or until nicely browned.
3. Cook remaining beef pieces in the same manner, then transfer into a bowl, add onions into the pot and cook for 5 minutes or until sauté.
4. Add carrots, season with paprika and onion soup mix, drizzle with Worcestershire sauce and pour in beef broth.
5. Return beef pieces into the instant pot, stir until just mixed and press the cancel button.
6. Shut the instant pot with its lid, turn the pressure knob to seal the pot, press the 'meat/stew' button, then press the 'timer' to set the cooking time to 20 minutes and cook at high pressure, instant pot will take 5 minutes or more for building its inner pressure.

7. When the timer beeps, press 'cancel' button and do natural pressure release for 10 minutes and then do quick pressure release until pressure nob drops down.
8. Open the instant pot, stir the stew and press the 'sauté/simmer' button.
9. Stir together cornstarch and water until combined, add to the instant pot, stir well and cook for 3 minutes or more until cooking sauce is thick to the desired level.
10. Serve straight away.

Beef Fajitas

Servings: 4
Preparation time: 15 minutes
Cooking time: 10 minutes

Nutrition Value:

Calories: 123 Cal, Carbs: 9 g, Fat: 3 g, Protein: 14 g, Fiber: 2 g.

Ingredients:

- 1-pound steak roast
- 1 medium red onion, peeled and cut into strips
- 1 medium red bell pepper, deseeded and cut into strips
- 1 medium yellow bell pepper, deseeded and cut into strips
- 1 tablespoon taco seasoning
- 2 limes, juiced and zest
- 1/2 cup beef stock

Method:

1. Cut beef into thin strips and season well with taco seasoning until evenly coated.
2. Plugin instant pot, insert the inner pot, add seasoned beef strips along with remaining onion, peppers and beef stock.
3. Shut the instant pot with its lid, turn the pressure knob to seal the pot, press the 'manual' button, then press the 'timer' to set the cooking time to 5 minutes and cook at high pressure, instant pot will take 5 minutes or more for building its inner pressure.
4. When the timer beeps, press 'cancel' button and do natural pressure release for 10 minutes and then do quick pressure release until pressure nob drops down.
5. Open the instant pot, add lime juice and zest into beef fajitas and stir until mixed.
6. Serve straight away.

Pork Chops

Servings: 2
Preparation time: 10 minutes
Cooking time: 22 minutes

Nutrition Value:

Calories: 354 Cal, Carbs: 24.5 g, Fat: 16.3 g, Protein: 27.9 g, Fiber: 2 g.

Ingredients:

- 2 boneless pork chops, each about 1-inch thick
- 1/2 teaspoon onion powder
- 1 teaspoon salt
- 1 teaspoon ground black pepper
- 2 tablespoons brown sugar
- 1 teaspoon paprika
- 1 tablespoon butter
- 1/2 tablespoon Worcestershire sauce
- 1 cup chicken broth
- 1 teaspoon liquid smoke

Method:

1. Stir together onion powder, salt, black pepper, sugar, and paprika and rub this mixture on all sides of pork chops until evenly coated.
2. Plugin instant pot, insert the inner pot, press sauté/simmer button, add butter and when it melts, add seasoned pork chops and cook for 2 minutes per side until browned.
3. Press the cancel button, add remaining ingredients and stir until mixed.
4. Shut the instant pot with its lid, turn the pressure knob to seal the pot, press the 'manual' button, then press the 'timer' to set the cooking time to 7 minutes and cook at high pressure, instant pot will take 5 minutes or more for building its inner pressure.
5. When the timer beeps, press 'cancel' button and do natural pressure release for 10 minutes and then do quick pressure release until pressure nob drops down.
6. Open the instant pot, transfer pork chops to a serving plate and let rest for 5 minutes.
7. Drizzle cooking sauce from the instant pot over pork chops and serve straight away.

Mustard Pork Chops

Servings: 4
Preparation time: 10 minutes
Cooking time: 25 minutes

Nutrition Value:

Calories: 165 Cal, Carbs: 9 g, Fat: 5 g, Protein: 19 g, Fiber: 0 g.

Ingredients:

- 4 pork chops, each about 1-inch thick
- 2 tablespoons salt
- 1 tablespoon ground black pepper
- 2 tablespoons honey
- 15-ounce mustard barbecue sauce, unsweetened
- 1 cup water

Method:

1. Plugin instant pot, insert the inner pot, add honey, barbecue sauce and water and whisk until mixed.
2. Season pork chops with salt and black pepper, then add to the instant pot, shut the instant pot with its lid and turn the pressure knob to seal the pot.
3. Press the 'manual' button, then press the 'timer' to set the cooking time to 15 minutes and cook at high pressure, instant pot will take 5 minutes or more for building its inner pressure.
4. When the timer beeps, press 'cancel' button and do quick pressure release until pressure nob drops down.
5. Open the instant pot, press the 'sauté/simmer' button and cook for 5 minutes or until cooking sauce in instant pot is reduce by half.
6. Press the cancel button, transfer pork chops to serving plates and ladle cooking sauce over it.
7. Serve straight away.

Pork Carnitas

Servings: 6
Preparation time: 15 minutes
Cooking time: 50 minutes

Nutrition Value:

Calories: 318 Cal, Carbs: 24 g, Fat: 12 g, Protein: 32 g, Fiber: 4 g.

Ingredients:

- 4 pounds boneless pork shoulder, cut into 3-inch pieces
- 3 teaspoons minced garlic
- 1 1/2 teaspoons salt
- 1/2 teaspoon ground black pepper
- 2 teaspoons red chili powder
- 2 teaspoons dried oregano
- 1 1/2 teaspoons ground cumin
- 1/4 cup lime juice, fresh
- 1 tablespoon olive oil
- 1/2 cup orange juice, fresh
- 12-ounce beef broth
- Tortillas for serving

Method:

1. Plugin instant pot, insert the inner pot, press sauté/simmer button, add oil and when hot, add pork pieces in a single layer and cook for 3 to 4 minutes per side or until nicely browned.
2. Cook remaining pieces in the same manner, then return browned pork pieces into the instant pot and add remaining ingredients.
3. Press the cancel button, shut the instant pot with its lid and turn the pressure knob to seal the pot.
4. Press the 'manual' button, then press the 'timer' to set the cooking time to 30 minutes and cook at high pressure, instant pot will take 5 minutes or more for building its inner pressure.
5. When the timer beeps, press 'cancel' button and do quick pressure release until pressure nob drops down.
6. Open the instant pot, shred pork with two forks and stir until mixed.
7. Serve pork with tortillas.

Rosemary Leg of Lamb

Servings: 8
Preparation time: 10 minutes
Cooking time: 55 minutes

Nutrition Value:

Calories: 432 Cal, Carbs: 1.02 g, Fat: 25.8 g, Protein: 44.7 g, Fiber: 0.4 g.

Ingredients:

- 4 pounds boneless leg of lamb
- 2 teaspoons minced garlic
- 2 teaspoons salt
- 1 ½ teaspoon ground black pepper
- 2 tablespoons chopped rosemary
- 2 tablespoons avocado oil, divided
- 2 cups water

Method:

1. Rinse leg of lamb, pat dry and then season with salt and black pepper.
2. Plugin instant pot, insert the inner pot, press sauté/simmer button, add oil and when hot, add a seasoned leg of lamb and cook for 4 to 5 minutes per side or until nicely browned.
3. Press the cancel button, pour in water, add garlic and rosemary, and insert trivet stand.
4. Place leg of lamb on the stand, shut the instant pot with its lid and turn the pressure knob to seal the pot.
5. Press the 'manual' button, then press the 'timer' to set the cooking time to 35 minutes and cook at high pressure, instant pot will take 5 minutes or more for building its inner pressure.
6. When the timer beeps, press 'cancel' button and do natural pressure release for 10 minutes and then do quick pressure release until pressure nob drops down.
7. Open the instant pot, transfer leg of lamb to a cutting board and let cool for 10 minutes.
8. Slice leg of lamb and serve.

Lamb Steaks

Servings: 4
Preparation time: 15 minutes
Cooking time: 50 minutes

Nutrition Value:

Calories: 178 Cal, Carbs: 3 g, Fat: 11 g, Protein: 15 g, Fiber: 0.9 g.

Ingredients:

- 1½ pound lamb steak
- 1 medium white onion, peeled and minced
- 2 teaspoons minced garlic
- 1 teaspoon grated ginger
- 1 ½ teaspoon salt
- 1 tablespoon sugar
- 1 teaspoon ground black pepper
- 3 tablespoons sesame oil
- ¼ cup soy sauce
- 2 tablespoons lemon juice
- 1 cup water
- 1 tablespoon corn starch

Method:

1. Plugin instant pot, insert the inner pot, press sauté/simmer button, add oil and when hot, add lamb steak and cook for 3 minutes per side or until nicely browned.
2. Add onion, garlic, and ginger and continue cooking for 2 minutes.
3. Add remaining ingredients except for cornstarch, then press the cancel button, shut the instant pot with its lid and turn the pressure knob to seal the pot.
4. Press the 'manual' button, then press the 'timer' to set the cooking time to 30 minutes and cook at high pressure, instant pot will take 5 minutes or more for building its inner pressure.
5. When the timer beeps, press 'cancel' button and do natural pressure release for 10 minutes and then do quick pressure release until pressure nob drops down.
6. Open the instant pot, transfer lamb steaks to a plate and keep warm.
7. Press the sauté/simmer button, stir cornstarch into the cooking sauce in instant pot and cook for 3 to 5 minutes or until thickened to desired consistency.
8. Drizzle sauce over lamb steaks and serve.

Chili Lime Steak Bowl

Servings: 6
Preparation time: 15 minutes
Cooking time: 22 minutes

Nutrition Value:

Calories: 437 Cal, Carbs: 15.1 g, Fat: 26.2 g, Protein: 35.4 g, Fiber: 0 g.

Ingredients:

- 2 pounds steaks, cut into strips
- 1 teaspoon minced garlic
- ½ teaspoon salt
- ½ teaspoon ground black pepper
- ½ teaspoon red chili powder
- 1 teaspoon hot sauce
- 2 teaspoons lime juice
- 1 tablespoon olive oil
- 1 tablespoon water
- 3 mediums avocado, pitted and flesh diced

Method:

1. Plugin instant pot, insert the inner pot, press sauté/simmer button, add oil and when hot, add garlic and cook for 1 minute or until fragrant.
2. Then add remaining ingredients except for avocado and stir until mixed.
3. Press the cancel button, shut the instant pot with its lid and turn the pressure knob to seal the pot.
4. Press the 'manual' button, then press the 'timer' to set the cooking time to 10 minutes and cook at high pressure, instant pot will take 5 minutes or more for building its inner pressure.
5. When the timer beeps, press 'cancel' button and do quick pressure release until pressure nob drops down.
6. Open the instant pot, press the 'sauté/simmer' button and cook for 5 minutes or until cooking sauce is reduce by half.
7. Evenly divide steaks between serving plates and serve with avocado.

Balsamic Beef Pot Roast

Servings: 3
Preparation time: 15 minutes
Cooking time: 50 minutes

Nutrition Value:

Calories: 322 Cal, Carbs: 4 g, Fat: 20 g, Protein: 32 g, Fiber: 4 g.

Ingredients:

- 3 pounds chuck roast, boneless
- 1/2 cup chopped white onion
- 1 teaspoon garlic powder
- 1 tablespoon salt
- 1 teaspoon black ground pepper
- 1/4 teaspoon xanthan gum
- 1/4 cup balsamic vinegar
- 1 tablespoon olive oil
- 2 cups beef broth
- 2 tablespoons chopped parsley

Method:
1. Stir together garlic, salt, and black pepper and rub this mixture on all sides of roast until evenly coated.
2. Plugin instant pot, insert the inner pot, press sauté/simmer button, add oil and when hot, add seasoned roast and cook for 4 minutes per side or until nicely golden brown.
3. Add remaining ingredients except for xanthan gum and parsley, stir until mixed and press the cancel button.
4. Shut the instant pot with its lid, turn the pressure knob to seal the pot, press the 'manual' button, then press the 'timer' to set the cooking time to 30 minutes and cook at high pressure, instant pot will take 5 minutes or more for building its inner pressure.
5. When the timer beeps, press 'cancel' button and do natural pressure release for 10 minutes and then do quick pressure release until pressure nob drops down.
6. Open the instant pot, transfer roast to a plate and break into bite-size pieces.
7. Press the 'sauté/simmer' button, add xanthan gum into the instant pot and cook for 3 to 5 minutes or until cooking sauce is reduced by half.
8. Return beef into the instant pot, stir until just mixed and press the cancel button.
9. Garnish beef with parsley and serve.

Chapter 11: Desserts

Carrot Cake

Servings: 6
Preparation time: 10 minutes
Cooking time: 55 minutes

Nutrition Value:

Calories: 139 Cal, Carbs: 17.3 g, Fat: 5 g, Protein: 5.8 g, Fiber: 2.6 g.

Ingredients:

For Cake:

- 2 cups grated carrots
- 1 banana, mashed
- 1 1/2 cup whole-meal flour
- ¼ cup sultanas
- 2 teaspoons mixed spice
- 1 teaspoon baking powder
- 3 tablespoons swerve sweetener
- ¼ cup rapeseed oil
- 3 eggs, slightly beaten
- 1 cup water

For Frosting:

- 1 orange, zested
- 1 ¼ cup cream cheese, fat-free
- 1 tablespoon swerve sweetener

Method:

1. Place flour in a bowl, add mixed spice and baking powder and stir until mixed.
2. Crack eggs in another bowl, add banana and beat the mixture until well combined.
3. Then beat in sweetener and oil until incorporated and then stir in flour mixture, 4 tablespoons at a time, until incorporated and smooth batter comes together.
4. Fold carrots and sultanas into the cake batter, then spoon the mixture into a greased cake pan and cover with aluminum foil.

5. Plugin instant pot, insert the inner pot, pour in water, then insert trivet stand and place the cake pan on it.
6. Shut the instant pot with its lid, turn the pressure knob to seal the pot, press the 'steam' button, then press the 'timer' to set the cooking time to 50 minutes and cook at high pressure, instant pot will take 5 minutes or more for building its inner pressure.
7. Meanwhile, prepare frosting and for this, beat together orange zest, cream cheese and swerve sweetener until smooth and chill it in the refrigerator until required.
8. When the timer beeps, press 'cancel' button and do quick pressure release until pressure nob drops down.
9. Open the instant pot, take out the cake, uncover it, and let the cake cool on wire rack.
10. Then transfer cake to a plate, spread prepared cream cheese frosting on tip and slice to serve.

Apple and Cinnamon Cake

Servings: 8
Preparation time: 10 minutes
Cooking time: 65 minutes
Nutrition Value:
Calories: 275 Cal, Carbs: 35 g, Fat: 14 g, Protein: 2 g, Fiber: 1 g.
Ingredients:

- 3 large apples, peeled, cored and diced
- 1/2 tablespoon ground cinnamon
- ¾ cup and 2 tablespoons swerve sweetener
- 1 1/2 cups flour and more as needed
- 1/2 tablespoon baking powder
- 1/2 teaspoon salt
- 1/2 cup olive oil
- 1 teaspoon vanilla extract, unsweetened
- 2 eggs
- 1 cup water

Method:

1. Place diced apples in a bowl, add cinnamon and 2 tablespoons sweetener and toss until evenly coated, set aside until required.
2. Place flour in a large bowl, add salt and baking powder and stir until mixed.
3. Crack eggs in another bowl, add vanilla, oil and remaining sugar and beat until well combined.
4. Then stir in flour mixture, 4 tablespoons at a time, until incorporated and then pour half of this mixture into a greased 7-inch cake pan.
5. Spread half of the apples on the batter in a cake pan, then pour remaining batter on the apple pieces and scatter remaining apples on top along with any juices.
6. Plugin instant pot, insert the inner pot, pour in water, and insert a steamer basket.
7. Cover cake pan with aluminum foil, then place it on the steamer basket, shut the instant pot with its lid and turn the pressure knob to seal the pot.
8. Press the 'manual' button, then press the 'timer' to set the cooking time to 60 minutes and cook at high pressure, instant pot will take 5 minutes or more for building its inner pressure.
9. When the timer beeps, press 'cancel' button and do quick pressure release until pressure nob drops down.
10. Open the instant pot, take out the cake pan, uncover it, and let the cake cool on wire rack.
11. Slice the cake and serve.

Poached Spiced Pears

Servings: 4
Preparation time: 15 minutes
Cooking time: 12 minutes

Nutrition Value:

Calories: 136 Cal, Carbs: 22 g, Fat: 0.2 g, Protein: 0.6 g, Fiber: 9 g.

Ingredients:

- 4 medium pears, peeled
- 1 lemon, juiced
- 1-star anise
- 1 stick of cinnamon
- 3 cups white grape juice
- 3½ cups water

Method:

1. Plugin instant pot, insert the inner pot, add all the ingredients except for pears and stir until just mixed.
2. Then add pears, shut the instant pot with its lid and turn the pressure knob to seal the pot.
3. Press the 'manual' button, then press the 'timer' to set the cooking time to 8 minutes and cook at high pressure, instant pot will take 5 minutes or more for building its inner pressure.
4. When the timer beeps, press 'cancel' button and do natural pressure release for 10 minutes and then do quick pressure release until pressure nob drops down.
5. Open the instant pot, transfer pears to serving plates and drizzle with cooking liquid.
6. Serve straight away.

Brownies

Servings: 16
Preparation time: 15 minutes
Cooking time: 55 minutes

Nutrition Value:

Calories: 200 Cal, Carbs: 24 g, Fat: 11 g, Protein: 2 g, Fiber: 1 g.

Ingredients:
- 3/4 cup whole wheat flour
- 1/2 teaspoon salt
- 1/2 teaspoon baking powder
- 1/2 cup cocoa powder, unsweetened
- 1 cup swerve sweetener
- 1 cup chocolate chips, unsweetened
- 1 teaspoon vanilla extract, unsweetened
- 1/2 cup butter, soften
- 2 eggs
- 1 ½ cup water

Method:
1. Place butter in a bowl, cream with a beater, then beat in sweetener until combined and beat in eggs and vanilla until incorporated.
2. Place flour in a bowl, add salt, baking powder, cocoa powder and stir until combined.
3. Stir the flour mixture into the egg mixture, 2 tablespoons at a time, until incorporated and then fold in chocolate chips until combined.
4. Take a 7 by 3 push pan or pan that fits into the instant pot, grease it with oil, then spoon in prepared batter, smooth the top and cover with aluminum foil.
5. Plugin instant pot, insert the inner pot, pour in water, insert trivet stand and place brownie pan on it.
6. Shut the instant pot with its lid, turn the pressure knob to seal the pot, press the 'manual' button, then press the 'timer' to set the cooking time to 50 minutes and cook at high pressure, instant pot will take 5 minutes or more for building its inner pressure.
7. When the timer beeps, press 'cancel' button and do natural pressure release for 10 minutes and then do quick pressure release until pressure nob drops down.
8. Open the instant pot, remove the pan, uncover it and let brownies cool in pan on wire rack.
9. Cut brownies into squares and serve.

Oatmeal Bites

Servings: 12
Preparation time: 20 minutes
Cooking time: 15 minutes

Nutrition Value:

Calories: 36.7 Cal, Carbs: 6.2 g, Fat: 1 g, Protein: 1.2 g, Fiber: 0.7 g.

Ingredients:

- 1 cup mixed berries, slightly mashed
- 1 cup rolled oats
- 1/2 cup whole wheat flour
- 1/4 teaspoon salt
- 1 tablespoon brown sugar
- 1/2 teaspoon cinnamon
- 1 teaspoon baking powder
- 1/3 cup honey
- 4 eggs
- 1 cup water

Method:
1. Place oats and flour in a bowl, add salt, cinnamon and baking powder and stir until mixed.
2. Crack eggs in a bowl, add sugar and honey and beat until well combined.
3. Then fold in flour mixture, 4 tablespoons at a time, until incorporated and then fold in berries.
4. Take twelve egg molds, grease them with oil, and then fill each portion with a scoop of cookie mixture, about 3 tablespoons.
5. Plugin instant pot, insert the inner pot, pour in water, then insert steamer basket and place egg molds on it.
6. Shut the instant pot with its lid, turn the pressure knob to seal the pot, press the 'manual' button, then press the 'timer' to set the cooking time to 10 minutes and cook at high pressure, instant pot will take 5 minutes or more for building its inner pressure.
7. When the timer beeps, press 'cancel' button and do natural pressure release for 10 minutes and then do quick pressure release until pressure nob drops down.
8. Open the instant pot, transfer egg molds to a wire rack to cool oatmeal bites, then take them out and dust with powdered sweetener.
9. Serve straight away.

Lime Curd

Servings: 3
Preparation time: 4 hours and 215 minutes
Cooking time: 15 minutes

Nutrition Value:

Calories: 45 Cal, Carbs: 8 g, Fat: 1 g, Protein: 1 g, Fiber: 0 g.

Ingredients:

- 2 teaspoons grated lime zest
- 1 cup swerve sweetener
- 2/3 cup lime juice
- 2 eggs
- 2 egg yolks
- 3-ounce butter, soften
- 1 ½ cup water

Method:

1. Place butter and sweetener in a bowl and beat for 2 minutes or until fluffy.
2. Then beat in eggs and egg yolks for 1 minute or until blended and then stir in lime juice until combined.
3. Plugin instant pot, insert the inner pot, pour in water, and insert a steamer basket.
4. Divide curd mixture evenly between three half-pint mason jars and place lids on them.
5. Place mason jars on the steamer basket, shut the instant pot with its lid and turn the pressure knob to seal the pot.
6. Press the 'manual' button, then press the 'timer' to set the cooking time to 10 minutes and cook at high pressure, instant pot will take 5 minutes or more for building its inner pressure.
7. When the timer beeps, press 'cancel' button and do natural pressure release for 10 minutes and then do quick pressure release until pressure nob drops down.
8. Open the instant pot, remove mason jars, then open carefully and stir lime zest into curd until mixed.
9. Close jars with the lid tightly and then cool in the refrigerator for 4 hours or overnight or until curd get thick.
10. Serve straight away.

Chocolate Pudding

Servings: 4
Preparation time: 4 hours and 15 minutes
Cooking time: 35 minutes

Nutrition Value:

Calories: 120 Cal, Carbs: 21 g, Fat: 3.5 g, Protein: 1 g, Fiber: 1 g.

Ingredients:

- 4 ounces unsweetened chocolate, chopped
- 1 tablespoon cocoa powder, unsweetened
- 1 teaspoon salt
- 1/3 cup brown sugar
- 1 teaspoon Vanilla extract, unsweetened
- 4 egg yolks
- 1 1/2 cups whipping cream, reduced fat
- 1 ¼ cups water

Method:

1. Place a saucepan over medium heat, add cream and heat for 3 to 4 minutes or until hot.
2. Then remove the pan from heat, add chocolate, then stir until chocolate melts and smooth mixture comes together.
3. Beat in remaining ingredients, except for water, and then strain the chocolate mixture into a round baking dish that fits into the instant pot.
4. Plugin instant pot, insert the inner pot, pour in water, and insert trivet stand.
5. Cover baking dish with aluminum foil, then place it on trivet stand, press the cancel button, shut the instant pot with its lid and turn the pressure knob to seal the pot.
6. Press the 'manual' button, then press the 'timer' to set the cooking time to 22 minutes and cook at low pressure, instant pot will take 5 minutes or more for building its inner pressure.
7. When the timer beeps, press 'cancel' button and do natural pressure release for 5 minutes and then do quick pressure release until pressure nob drops down.
8. Open the instant pot, remove baking dish and uncover it and let cool at room temperature.
9. Cover the baking dish and chill in the refrigerator for 4 hours or overnight and then serve.

Chocolate Fudge

Servings: 8
Preparation time: 4 hours and 10 minutes
Cooking time: 10 minutes

Nutrition Value:

Calories: 90 Cal, Carbs: 16.8 g, Fat: 3 g, Protein: 0.5 g, Fiber: 0.4 g.

Ingredients:

- 2 1/2 cups chocolate chips, unsweetened
- 1/8 teaspoon salt
- 2 teaspoons liquid stevia, vanilla flavored
- 1 teaspoon vanilla extract, unsweetened
- 1/3 cup coconut milk, reduced fat

Method:

1. Plugin instant pot, insert the inner pot, add all the ingredients, stir until just mixed, then press the 'sauté/simmer' button and whisk the mixture until well combined.
2. Press the cancel button, press the 'keep warm' button, and continue whisking the mixture until all chocolate chips are well melted.
3. Take a rimmed baking sheet, lined with aluminum foil, then grease with oil and pour in chocolate mixture.
4. Place the baking sheet into the refrigerator and chill for 4 hours or more until firm.
5. Cut fudge into square pieces and serve.

Conclusion

Diabetes is a common condition that can blood sugar level to go high. Early symptoms of diabetes include increased hunger and thirst, feeling fatigued, pain in hands and feet, more urination, yeast infection, and slow healing of wounds. The longer diabetes remains untreated, the risk of developing other health problems increases. Untreated diabetes leads to very high blood glucose level and severe hydration, which could trigger hyperosmolar hyperglycemic nonketotic syndrome (HHNS), which often leads to diabetic coma and eventually death. Anyone suffering from these symptoms should see the doctor immediately as these symptoms may lead to serious ailments. So, call your doctor if you:

- Feel weak, sick to your stomach and very thirsty
- Frequently peering
- Bad stomach ache
- Breathing faster and deeper than normal
- The breath which smells like nail polish remover

The early detection of diabetes, starting its treatment, and monitoring sugar levels improves the quality of life of a diabetic and significantly reduces the risk of severe diseases.

CPSIA information can be obtained
at www.ICGtesting.com
Printed in the USA
LVHW101345010221
678013LV00004B/29

9 781953 702555